FACE TO FACE WITH FACTS

THE ART OF READING FACES

HERMANN MÜLLER

OVER 300 ILLUSTRATIONS

© Copyright 2002 Hermann Müller. All rights reserved.

No part of this publication may be reproduced, stored in a retrieval system, or transmitted, in any form or by any means, electronic, mechanical, photocopying, recording, or otherwise, without the written prior permission of the author.

Printed in Victoria, Canada

Illustrations and book design
by Herman Müller
Photographs by Steve Holland

Contact for Herman Müller
Email: harmony@qldnet.com.au

Website
http://www.harmony.au.com

National Library of Canada Cataloguing in Publication Data

Müller, Hermann, 1936-
    Face to face with facts / Hermann Müller.
ISBN 1-55395-354-1
    1. Personality assessment.   I. Title.
BF176.M84 2003   155.2   C2002-905555-5

TRAFFORD

This book was published *on-demand* in cooperation with Trafford Publishing.
On-demand publishing is a unique process and service of making a book available for retail sale to the public taking advantage of on-demand manufacturing and Internet marketing. **On-demand publishing** includes promotions, retail sales, manufacturing, order fulfilment, accounting and collecting royalties on behalf of the author.

Suite 6E, 2333 Government St., Victoria, B.C. V8T 4P4, CANADA
   Phone   250-383-6864   Toll-free 1-888-232-4444 (Canada & US)
   Fax   250-383-6804   E-mail   sales@trafford.com
   Web site   www.trafford.com   TRAFFORD PUBLISHING IS A DIVISION OF TRAFFORD HOLDINGS LTD.
   Trafford Catalogue #02-1069   www.trafford.com/robots/02-1069.html

    10   9   8   7   6   5   4   3

ACKNOWLEDGEMENTS

My first acknowledgement must go to my father who was renowned as an artist for over 60 years. He captured impressions of people's faces so perfectly that my fascination for the expressions on faces were imprinted in me as long ago as I can remember. My mother and sisters are artists too.

I learnt to look at people straight in the eyes and study their faces, unconsciously interested. For this I must thank every Soul I have met for they have taught me something: everyone is very interesting. The many countries I have travelled and worked in has made this work unfold so well.

My special thanks goes to my photographer friend Steve Holland, who has provided so many beautiful and interesting photographs presented in this book. I thank the owner of every face that is used here, fully or in part. They all participate, with me, in creating a better understanding of life. That is the purpose of this book.

I thank Marie, my wife, for her patience and perseverance that has been an inspiration to me. Her support has been invaluable while I compiled this book.

The many hours of editing and pre-print preparation that is indispensable must be accounted for. I, thank my daughter Gillian Maddigan especially for this work. I also thank Sophia Shenandoah for her work and advice and Darryl Butler, who has assisted with his professional guidance.

My daughter Gillian has become an excellent face reader and I am inspired by many others I have taught, who are using this work professionally. I wish to include some of the people that have promoted my seminars and workshops and made this compassionate science available to thousands of others.

I wish to express my special thanks to some of my many networkers:
Alison Quedly, Karen Mills, New Zealand; Gerda Breustedt, Hille Lerbs, Waltraud Brix, Germany; Lilli Ann Whittall, Carole Friesen, Lee Ann Nicholson, Troi Lenard, Canada: Lyn Johnson, USA; Trish Lyth, UK; Katirina Sandstrom, Eva Sjöde, Sweden; Marie Müller, Cheri Hall, Australia.

Face to Face with Facts

Disclaimer

This is a teaching manual designed in the simplest and most basic way. I have as far as possible attempted to use real people. We are here to learn from so many that have set examples by their achievements in life. I have endeavoured to present, with the most positive description, the way they have used potentials of their personalities to achieve what they have. For this I, and all who read this book, must thank them for how they give us this opportunity to learn.

The first principle of Face Reading is to understand people for who they are, potentially, and what they are as a result of their interaction in life. We are all just as human as they are. Look at what the particular feature is contributing to the whole person. That is only a part of the person. There may be many other attributes that counteract or add to the individual part you notice.

The second principle is to enhance communication and to enrich the capacity of our interaction at the very first meeting, so our right to be human is respected and accepted by those around us. This is my contribution towards opening up boundaries created by nationalities, religious beliefs, ethnic and civil laws. I trust that this will enable us to be a free soul with its right to be an individual.

This book is created for your learning experience. The comments are only a point of view and my observation. I ask that every word here is accepted as an opinion only. I have also learnt from many other authors that have made very valuable contributions to this art of face reading. I recommend that you read some of them to add to what I have presented here.

You are free to accept or reject any of the comments made in this book. As the author I assume no responsibility to any person with respect to any damage alleged to be caused by the comments, illustrations or information presented in this book.

Hermann Müller

Contents

Foreword *by Hermann Müller*   vi
Introduction   viii

Part 1: The Art of Reading Faces is a Science

Communication is the Key   2
The Face at First Glance   4
Structure and Shape indicates Performance   7
Basic Structures and Combinations   11

Part 2: Assessment of the Individual Parts

The Forehead - *Frame of the Mind*   22
The Eyebrows - *Communication*   29
The Eyes - *A Point of View*   33
The Nose - *The Personality Knows*   38
The Ear - *Listening Carefully*   43
The Cheeks and Cheekbones - *Cheekiness*   47
The Lips - *The Taste for Life*   49
The Jaw and Chin - *Vitality and Foundation*   52
Lines of Development - *Tell Tale Lines*   54
Facial Hair - *Grounding and Sensitivity*   58

Part 3: Identification of Potentialities

Potentials - Intellectual, Financial or Physical   66
Reliability & Determination   70
Projection of the Personality   71
Creativity, Memory & Intuition   72
Self Control & Spontaneity   73
Love & Sensuality   74
Health, Vitality & Longevity   75
Happiness & Emotional Stability   76

Part 4: Notable Personalities ~ Case Studies

How to to Read a Face   78
Mother Theresa   79
Princess Diana   80
Bill Clinton   81
Bob Ansett   82
George Bush   83
Two Faces of Adolf Hitler   84
Conclusion   84

Appendix:

Quick Chart Reference
Index

Foreword

Everything I need to know about myself or another person is written in the face. It fascinates me to look at someone and realise that all I choose to know is facing me like an open book willing to be read. Since I have learnt to read faces, my life and understanding of others has changed dramatically. I am at home with myself and other people feel at home with me.

Each face I look at is saying to me......

"Please understand and accept me for who I am. This is how I experience my world, which is different from yours. To communicate effectively I need to see, hear and feel you with a deep understanding to savour the fullness of this meeting. What an amazing feeling it is to look deep into your true essence and you look into mine."

This is indeed a unique feeling. I feel very privileged that I can experience this magic any time I choose as a Face Reader and understand the potential of anyone's personality.

I have travelled and worked in many different countries. Asia, Europe, Papua New Guinea, Canada, the USA, Australia and New Zealand. Each country has their individual racial, cultural and language differences, however, they all have a common denominator, their human nature. It is not the words spoken but the language of the structure and performance of their facial features and their sensory responses to life that speaks their truth. This is portraying their intrinsic qualities expressed or suppressed and their frame of mind, emotions and purpose.

As a Face Character Analyst I have read thousands of faces in all of these places professionally. I feel quite at home wherever I am and whoever I am with. This immediate knowing that comes from years of observation, training and teaching this subject has added a fullness and freedom to my life that is so exciting. I wish to share this with as many people as possible. When, I am at ease with knowing who I am, those I am with feel at ease with me. Communication then flows freely in harmony and cooperation.

Foreword

The Art of Reading Faces provides us with a good opportunity to make our life more interesting and exciting. Face reading is the most natural thing we do. We unconsciously feel an attraction or a caution when confronted by someone new. Why not learn to recognise people consciously? We can then be more precise and get the best out of every situation.

This book is a learning and teaching manual. I have designed it to recognise the basics first. You then flesh out the individual responses and build a full characteristic understanding of an individual. You will deepen your perception and feelings of others and awaken the depth of your own intuition. The tangible proof of what you notice becomes undeniable and the reality of life unfolds in front of you. You will experience your loved ones, friends, those at work, people in the movies or on TV, the news and those on the street in a fascinating way you may never have noticed before. Your world will never be the same again.

"Face To Face with Facts" gives you the factual tools to be very accurate in your assessment of the individual in front of you. The potential of the personality is clearly etched in the face. Everyone I have read, without exception, has been amazed at how much information about them was so obvious to me.

I have often heard this feedback :"How do you know so much about me and my life when we have never met before? You have told me so many things that I have secretly known inside about myself but I never believed because no-one has recognised it. Your acceptance of me the way I am has been such a gift to me. I can now accept myself for who I am."

From the earliest days of our lives we have been subjected to the expectations and judgement of others. This separates us from identifying with ourselves. Here is the opportunity to give back to a person their birthright, the freedom to be who they really are.

I love this work. To look into the very essence of a soul with love, compassion and total acceptance is a personal healing experience. I wish to share this opportunity with those who choose to care for others.

Hermann

Introduction

Come **"Face to Face with Facts"** by studying **Personology**. The art of reading the potential characteristics of a personality is a very exact science. The simplicity in the application of these principles gives the trained personologist the capacity to quickly access a vast amount of information about the characteristics of the person observed.

A camera photographs the face of a person visually. This frozen image at that instant of stillness can be studied later in great detail. While observing the same person, the human intelligence imprints within the observer, a continuous stream of information through all five senses. This is retained within the observer creating a series of reactions that are constantly being instinctively assessed and evaluated by the subconscious mind and retained as cellular memory. Every part of the bodymind is in the face, therefore in that instant everything about the observed person is recorded by the observer.

What is it we do with this information? Our mind, like quicksilver, instantly flits from one thing to another distracted by our own thoughts and so many other things around us. The conscious mind then labours, slowly analysing with the memory of the past to reason with the present. That precious moment of total information is lost, glossed over by a hundred other imprints and sensory responses that confuses our understanding of each other.

This work has been organised to provide a systematic process of reading fundamental characteristics that provide the framework for application to any one of the billion variations of faces and people we may come across. Each of the four parts of this book gives you the opportunity to assess quickly the overall picture, individual characteristics, emotional traits, and the presentation of the tangible facts that create a full case history of *his story*. You will notice the individuality of the other and a depth of feeling in yourself. You can only be in touch with your own feelings and responses to the other person. To understand that person then, you must get deeper into yourself. The deeper you go into yourself the more you get to know yourself. This is a very nurturing experience. This is the key to even greater self-confidence.

Introduction

Features get etched into the face to show habitual performance, thoughts and desires that create facial structure and leave tell-tale lines. A cartoonist is a good personologist. With a few specific lines he depicts the character of a known personality by exaggerating some of the person's outstanding facial features. Most people then recognise them immediately.

The Art of Reading a Personality's Potential is an essential tool in this new millennium of communication and efficiency. The sensitivity for a deep understanding of each other brings a great deal of peace, cooperation and success to all that we do in every area of life. This is the science of **Personology**.

Movie-makers choose actors who have the special characteristics that suit the personality of the role they have to play to make it flow naturally. We get attracted or repelled by this subtle transference of information from one to another when we come face to face with them. Certain characteristics of the person before us become apparent and need to be understood before appointing her to a responsible position. We learn to make friends and understand our relationships better by this unspoken language of facing each other. As we improve our sense of discernment of a sales person or client's potential, we have greater success in our transactions.

Rather than be driven by opinions and past negative experiences, utilise the tangible facts by reading what is staring at you in the face and giving you all the information you need to make the right decision. Come *Face to Face with the Facts* and use the personality's potential. Live in the present moment. Utilise this information to the fullest. This puts you a step ahead of the other person and creates the cutting edge that makes the difference in all that you do in your life.

"Being alive is the greatest miracle on earth.
Let us enjoy it with the fullest awareness in every moment of our life."

The best gift of all, of course, is to just care enough to understand.

Personology

The Communication Tool of the New Millennium
Assessment of Personality Potential

Human Resource Professionals	Senior & Middle Management
Public Relations Personnel	Consultants ~ Politicians ~ Diplomats
Psychiatrists ~ Therapists	Parents ~ Teachers ~ Counsellors
Theatre ~ Talent Scouts	Salesmen ~ Receptionists ~ Physicians
Know Your Family and Friends	Doctors ~ Nurses ~ Social Workers

Everyday Applications of Personology

Improving Relationships	Negotiating
Interviewing	Team Building
Sales Performances	Job Interviews
Leading Seminars	Understanding the Audience
Effective Management	Staff Interaction
Selecting Personal Partners	Business Relationships

Part 1

The Art of Reading Faces is a Science

Communication is the Key

The Face at First Glance

Structure and Shape indicates Performance

Basic Structures and Combinations

Accept me for who I am

*The greatest gift of all, of course, is to just care enough
to understand.
This is my experience of Love*

Part 1:
The Art of Reading Faces is a Science

Communication is the Key

Technological Communication

Auckland - New Zealand

In every part of the world there has been a phenomenal growth and progress in almost every field of human endeavour. The creative mind is stimulated by every type of new information available to it. The global internet continues to double the web of our communication each day. Just a decade ago, very few of us could even imagine the technology we use today. These quantum leaps of continuing progress, facilitated by the instant availability of information, is constantly being assimilated and improved upon as if our very survival depended on it.

Inter-Personal Communication

Calgary - Canada

Communication is the key factor. Yes, so it is. Our very survival in this world depends on keeping up with this process of quickening, constantly being aware of what is happening out there to be in this human race. Most often, when we are so caught up in this maze of changing information around us, we forget our internal sensory communication systems. We then lose touch with ourselves and those around us. This leaves us cool and unaware of our own bodies and of everybody else.

Calgary - Canada

Body Mind Communication has become a prerequisite for any further improvement in relationships with ourselves and others to keep pace with this changing world. The purpose of reading faces is to recognise, understand and respond to ourselves and others immediately at the moment of contact. We understand a long-time friend very well, yet we take so long to accept and understand someone we have met for the first time. It is only our resistance, insecurity or lack of attention that separates us from reading the language that their bodymind is communicating to us.

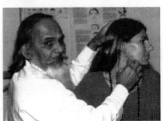

Gold Coast - Australia

Let us Face the Facts that I am so pleased to recognise the face of a friend I have not met in years, among a group of strangers in a foreign country. That friendly face suddenly seems to jump out among all the other faceless ones. All human beings are worthy of equal recognition and understanding.

Part 1: The Art of Reading Faces is a Science

It is so nurturing to look into the eyes of a person you have never met before with a warm smile of recognition. It sometimes comes like a shock to them to be worthy of the notice. You will start to recognise human beings wherever you go – in shopping malls, on the street, you may even get to know your neighbour after so many years. Watching the movies, the television, paging through magazines or noticing the characteristics of those standing for election will never be the same.

The Art of Reading Faces creates an atmosphere of comfort, acceptance and understanding at a subconscious level between the observed and the observer, even at the first meeting. This is an attitude of "I know you so well. It is so good to meet you again."

Vancouver - Canada

* *Those soft, warm brown eyes* or *steely-grey cold look*; *the rugged square jaw* or *the pointed chin* * *The furrowed thoughtful brow* or *the bland, colourless poker face* * *Those sensuously full lips, an inviting smile* or *the thin, tight, bitter taste of life* * *That honest, bold and steady gaze* or *the shifty or suspicious look*.

These characteristics are asking us to recognise them for who they are.

These common phrases

Nürnberg - Germany

In the most honest way the face says: "This is what I am, understand me and accept me in the only way I know, at this point of time. I am here to share this world with you as you do. There are very few people that have ever looked at me as closely and with the interest and understanding that you do. I thank you for this and for being my friend. Even those that have been with me for many years have not cared to notice me so closely as you do now. This is an unusual but fulfilling experience."

This is the kindliest act you can do for someone you have never met before. There are many more people who need kindness and recognition in this world. The boundaries of countries, religions and cultures are breaking down, allowing us to mix freely with each other and create a more harmonious world.

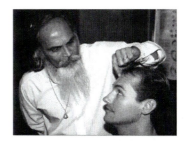

Gold Coast - Australia

The Face At First Glance

First Impressions

Read the "Head Lines"

The **first impression** I get of a person I have never met before is the most important. It is like picking up the Sunday newspaper and looking at the **headlines**. It catches my interest and then, I read the rest of the news in **smaller print** one paragraph at a time, to get the details until the whole story unfolds.

Overall Head Shape frontal and profile

I am first impressed by the **overall shape of the head** and **face** and the most prominent feature that jumps out at me and catches my attention. The overall structure supports the rest of the characteristics. The face shape may be square and practical, oval – sensitive and flexible, rectangular – steadfast and ambitious or round – easy-going and willing to please.

Most Prominent Feature

Her most **prominent feature** may be her warm, large brown eyes that catch my attention, a prominent nose that may be a bit nosey, or thin, tight lips that find life tastes very bitter. These prominent features may be one of her strongest personality traits that need to be noticed. They have left noticeable features on her face.

Frame of the Mind

After taking note of these **headlines**, I start to study each paragraph of the **news items**. I look at her **frame of the mind** indicated by the height and width of the forehead to note how broad and open-minded she is. In profile and front-on, I notice the proportion and priorities she has on observation, memory and imagination.

Eye Brows & Eyes

I notice the shape, placement and quality of the **eyebrows** to assess the degree of communication between her mental and emotional interaction. Their thickness angle and setting all have messages for me. Then I experience the special privilege of looking into the **eyes**, the windows to the very heart of her existence. Their size, shape, angle, depth, colour all indicate her point of view and how she expresses or suppresses her inner world and interacts with the outer environment. I act as the mirror so that she may see herself.

Nose, Mouth & Lips

The **nose** knows and shows how she has learnt to project her personal identity. Stability and steadfast, sharp and exacting, or prominent and outgoing, the nose points to honesty, dependability, self-confidence and strength. Her taste for life seen in the full and sensuous **lips**. The degree of creativity, intuition and sexual appeal is in the top lip. The fluent vocal expression in the bottom lip is supported by a large, relaxed smile. This one can be sweet and saucy.

Part 1: The Art of Reading Faces is a Science

The width and depth of the **jaw** and **chin** shows the stability, vitality, determination and capacity to carry through and support the expression of the above traits. With her prominent cheekbones, this sense of ambition and achievement will be well assured. Then we have the tell-tale lines etched into the face that tell us about the deeper feelings and habitual characteristics in the first few minutes as we come face to face.

Jaw, Chin & Cheekbones

'Tell-tale' **lines**

I know this person so well – better than she realises, and perhaps better than she is aware of herself. A deeper scrutiny will give me a wealth of information that may be invaluable to the relationship, whether it is business or friendship. This first meeting can make all the difference in our interactions. Most situations in life do not give us the opportunity for written psychological tests. This opportunity is too important to be lost.

"I know you at first glance"

Recognising Personalities on Sight.

There are some **special characteristics** about them that are impressed upon our memory that allows us to distinguish one person from the other.

Face to Face with Facts

The Face is the Autobiography of Life

Every part of the body is seen in the face. A careful study of the face shows how we utilise all these potential characteristics, creating a unique personality with all the facial features.

1.1 Front View ~ Facing the World

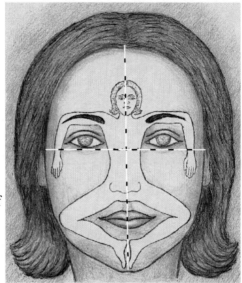

Right Side

Left Brain – Analytical ~ Personality ~ Mental

Male – Yang ~ Actions ~ Doing

Width of the Face from the Centreline shows the Adaptability and Expression of each relevant area of the Face

Yang

Left Side

Right Brain – Creative ~ Soul ~ Emotional

Female – Ying ~ Reactions Caring

Height of the Face from the Hairline to Chin tip shows the capacity of the three zones – Mental, Emotional and Physical

Yin

This is what I am, Body Mind and Soul. Understand me with Love and Compassion.

1.2 Profile ~ Projecting the Personality into the World

	Male ~ Action	**Female** ~ Reactions
Mental	Quick observant mind ready to act	Creative mind works behind the action
	Strong Ego ready to *go out there* Sharp and Precise	Emotions deeply recessed and well controlled
Physical	Quick reflexes with the mind ready to push for action	Sensuality carefully controlled by the mind

Part 1: The Art of Reading Faces is a Science

Structure and Shape Indicates Performance

Basic Face Shapes

The **Overall Face Structure** and **Shape** gives us a quick indication of the personality type in general. The **structure** is particularly suited for the **relevant performance** – it is like the blueprint, while the fleshing out and the individual parts give the distinguishing characteristics and personality to the face.

* **Focus completely** on what is in front of you;
* **Structural anatomy** is the foundation for emotional experience;
* **Let your sensory response** be your experience of their sensory expression;
* **Accept it** for what it is showing you. Do not analyse your opinions of it.

Some basic principles apply that may appropriately indicate the specific characteristics of each of these personality types. This indicates potential expression of energy and qualities.

Characteristics in General

Overall Structure and Face Shape

1.3 Easygoing, happy, very sensitive, easily influenced, nurturing and affectionate. This one often suppresses her own emotions and demands the attention of others. Is manipulative or can manipulate.

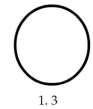

1.3

1.4 With her feminine sensitivity and softness, she is warm, idealistic, affectionate, caring for others and their point of view. Curved lines show the willingness to change and be flexible, though she will stand up for her ideals and inner values.

1.4

1.5 Solid, basic, down to earth, resolute, practical, less imaginative, this one is a doer rather than a thinker with a strong, earthy passion. He can be fiery by nature with physical vitality and a tendency to hold his ground.

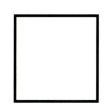

1.5

Face to Face with Facts

Overall Structure and Face Shape

Structure and Shape Indicates Performance
Characteristics in General

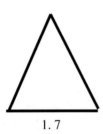
1.6

1.6 This one has high ideals – a humanitarian with an intellectual drive to represent these in life with the strength and the determination to stand up for them. He can be supportive, reliable, has good mental and emotional balance with good vitality to carry it out. With a high mental energy this one may need grounding.

1.7

1.7 Resolute and stubborn. This one can be unreasonable, introverted or closed-minded. He tends to have some frustration and anger from suppressed emotions. Vindictiveness could be a result of the fixed focus. He needs to be more relaxed and accepting of others' opinions.

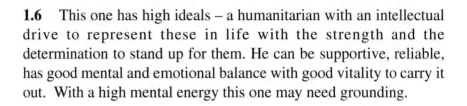
1.8

1.8 He is highly intellectual, very sensitive, quick and open-minded. He can be easily upset when misunderstood and needs grounding. The high mental energy could cause physical burn out and over-sensitivity.

Combinations of some of the above basic types

Most faces will have varying degrees of mixtures of the basic types in their overall structure. Study the combinations of the above noted characteristics to acknowledge the potential.

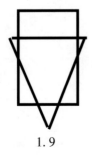
1.9

1.9 A combination of Figure 1.6 (high ideals and intellect) and Figure 1.8 (quite emotional and can be oversensitive and easily upset). This one is physically light and sensitive and needs to stay focused and centred.

Part 1: The Art of Reading Faces is a Science

Characteristics in General

Combinations of some of the above basic types

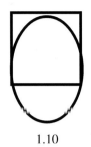
1.10

1.10 A combination of Figure 1.5 (solid, basic, shows practical thinking with a balanced emotional attitude) and Figure 1.4 (shows a softness and flexibility in interaction with others and self).

1.11

1.11 A combination Figure 1.7 (singleminded and internalises – thoughts and emotions) and Figure 1.5 (physical, earthy, can be stubborn and cautious).

Fundamentals of Basic Settings and Lines

The **frames** and **angles** of the settings of the various sensory organs in the face indicate the balance and ease of performance. The **lines** of the face are created by the repeated use of the muscle structure that etches them into the face indicating characteristics and attitudes of the person. These are distinguishing marks of the personality of the individual.

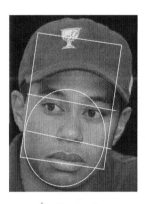
An Example

Bearing these tell-tale lines and shapes in mind, while observing the separate parts of the face, you get valuable information of the personality and habitual behaviour of the person. A cartoonist may use these very graphically to identify the character of an individual.

Characteristics in General

Tell-Tale Lines

1.12 A straightforward, practical and reliable person who could be inflexible and see things as black and white, especially indicated in hair line or eyebrow setting or the line of the lips. However, when noticed in the level of the eyes this indicates his emotional balance and the way he sees the world.

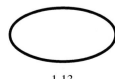
1.12

1.13 When the lines are curved, they indicate a flexible quality of one who is appreciative and open to change. This shows the flow of energy in a wave.

1.13

Face to Face with Facts

Characteristics in General

Tell-Tale Line

1.14

1.14 Right angular lines in the structure show this person is supportive, reliable and has strength, power and determination. He will stand up for his beliefs.

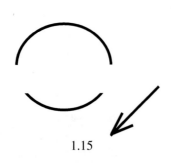
1.15

1.15 Descending lines at corners of the mouth, outer edges of the eyebrow or eyes show some depression, sadness or lack of cooperation. Drooping lines show a loss or suppression of energy.

1.16 Suppression, focus, mental control and frustration is experienced when these descending lines come together especially at the eyebrows, lips and hairline.

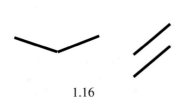
1.16

1.17 Rising, uplifting lines indicate power, happiness and hope. When the angle of the eyes are higher on the outside and slope down towards the nose this shows a mental or critical point of view.

1.17

1.18 When the eyebrow is pointed, it shows a sharp mental focus.

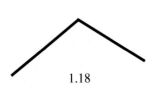
1.18

The Importance of Geometrical Patterns

The geometrical shapes all show the quality and quantity of energy flow from one zone to the other. The architecture of the "home" or "vehicle" of expression signifies the individuality of its performance according to its structural characteristics. It creates emanation or containment of sensory responses in the relevant areas of the face and therefore of the body-mind.

Basic Structures & Combinations

The Three Zones – Mental, Emotional and Physical

1.19 Three Zones and the Body in the Face

This diagram shows how the various parts of the psychosomatic responses of the Body-Mind are represented in the face. These features express or suppress our thoughts, feelings and emotional tension. The individual energy centres of the body are represented in each part of the face. They relate to our behaviour and attitude towards life.

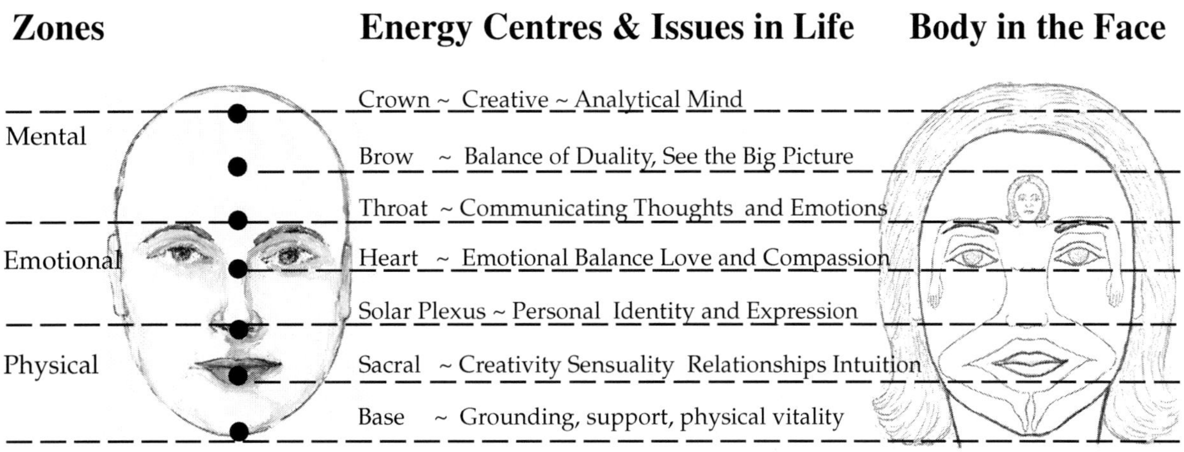

Zones	Energy Centres & Issues in Life	Body in the Face
Mental	Crown ~ Creative ~ Analytical Mind	
	Brow ~ Balance of Duality, See the Big Picture	
	Throat ~ Communicating Thoughts and Emotions	
Emotional	Heart ~ Emotional Balance Love and Compassion	
	Solar Plexus ~ Personal Identity and Expression	
Physical	Sacral ~ Creativity Sensuality Relationships Intuition	
	Base ~ Grounding, support, physical vitality	

In all faces observe the size and balance of the three zones:-
Note how the Issues in Life are being expressed by the separate parts

1. Compare the percentage of **mental, emotional, physical** volume of face exposed

2. Evaluate **Left** (emotional or soul) and **right** (mental or personality)

3. Study the **details** of the **separate parts** (refer Part 2)

4. Note the most **prominent feature**

5. Accept the **face presented.** Apply the **basic facts** to understand the potential

Face to Face with Facts

Basic Structures & Combinations

The Three Zones – Mental, Emotional and Physical

Case Study

1.20 Sizing up the Face at a glance

Overall face shape – Oval, Venus, Water
Sensitive, flexible, warm, affectionate and gentle.

Most prominent feature – Sensual lips
Nurturing sensitivity, good creativity and vocal expression. Both lips are full, well formed and relaxed.

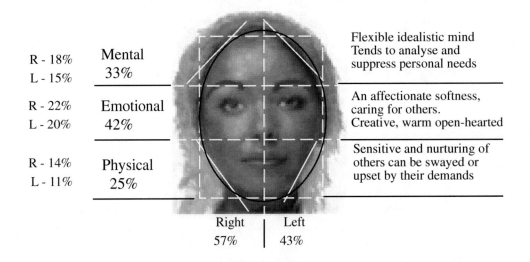

R - 18% Mental 33% — Flexible idealistic mind. Tends to analyse and suppress personal needs
L - 15%

R - 22% Emotional 42% — An affectionate softness, caring for others. Creative, warm open-hearted
L - 20%

R - 14% Physical 25% — Sensitive and nurturing of others can be swayed or upset by their demands
L - 11%

Right 57% | Left 43%

A typical Venus ~ Water person.

Notice the difference between the left /right sides.
The controlled left side shows some holding back of emotional expression seen in the less percentage of energy, the smaller and higher left eye with a slight tightening of the left corner of the mouth.

Part 1: The Art of Reading Faces is a Science

Basic Structures & Combinations

The structure of the overall face shape is the blueprint of the person's or soul's particular characteristics for its performance. The proportion of percentages of the **mental, emotional** and **physical** structure of the face gives a broad view of the personality type. The study of the separate parts and the fleshing out of the structure gives greater details of the expression of its personality.

1.21 A Comparative Chart of Overall Face Shapes

Some principal face shapes, metaphorically identified with different planets and relevant elements, can be used as a general guide to assess the characteristics within the face. Note area of the Mental - Emotional - Physical portions exposed. Percentages of each in relation to the others will give us a quick weighing up of the characteristic personality type of the face.

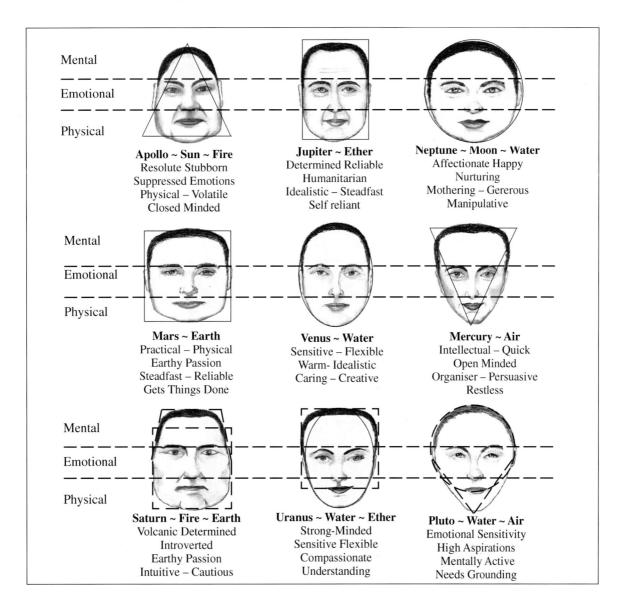

13

Face to Face with Facts

Basic Structures & Combinations

Fleshing Out The Framework

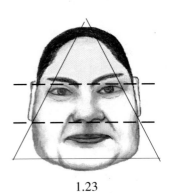
1.22

1.22 The face is the centre of the five senses. With 27 major muscles constantly at work acting and reacting to life and everything the bodymind is experiencing, we create a face that is unique and individual. Every mental and emotional reaction affects the biochemical structure in the muscle tissue and the sensory organs in the face. The repetitious patterns get ingrained, literally creating our specialised features, called character.

Common Characteristics of Basic Face Shapes

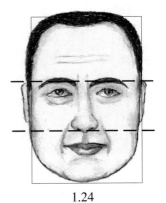
1.23

1.23 Apollo ~ Sun Fire. Resolute, stubborn, suppressed emotions, physically strong, closed mind.
The wide jaw and pointed forehead gives this one the characteristics of a fiery personality. This one could have ambition and drive but may lack patience. The aggressive nature can create an exaggerated need for control. He can be charming and pleasant when he chooses, backing the one that most suits his needs, or internalises his feelings when his demands are not met. The energy is strong in the physical zone. With a somewhat closed mind, he has an ambition and drive to satisfy his earthy desires with a stubborn persistence until they are fulfilled.

1.24 Jupiter ~ Ether. Determined, reliable, humanitarian, idealistic, steadfast, self-reliant.
Dignified and pleasant, this one has high ideals with the determination and strength to stand up for them. He is thoughtful, has great vision and the desire to uphold the law and the rights of others. With a high intellect he is *born to rise to high positions*. The qualities of thoughtfulness, optimism, strong ideals and unshakable fixity of purpose gains this one many friends and their love and respect. He needs to be aware of the possibility of these good qualities affecting the pride and the ego. The slight curve with the wide jaw shows the sensitivity is supported by an inner strength.

1.24

Part 1: The Art of Reading Faces is a Science

Basic Structures & Combinations

Common Characteristics of Basic Face Shapes

1.25 Neptune ~ Moon ~ Water. Affectionate, happy, nurturing, mothering, generous.
Warm, affectionate, easy-going, gentle, friendly and ready to help those in need. This round faced-person has a changeable nature. He can get easily bored, needs plenty of encouragement, avoids hard work and takes the line of least resistance, which could turn towards sluggishness. His physique usually tends towards chubbiness or excess weight. Due to the emotional sensitivity and the desire to be gentle to those on the outside, his psychosomatic response tends to hold the emotion and the tension that is deeply buried under the soft, outer desensitised tissue.

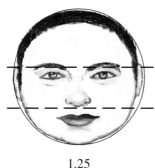
1.25

1.26 Mars ~ Earth. Practical, physical, earthy passion, steadfast, reliable, gets things done.
The Mars temperament signifies high energy, vitality and an aggressive, earthy personality. This one is practical and well grounded, a doer rather than a thinker. The forehead can tend to be wide but narrow, with a strong muscular body and good health. He tends to *shoot first and ask questions afterwards*, yet soon forgives and forgets. He has a sociable nature and has a love for the opposite sex. He is happy with his loved ones and unhappy when alone. His inner strength can be vulnerable, especially when left to his own devices, due to his melancholic temperament. The psychosomatic response is a muscular armouring covering a very sensitive, emotional nature.

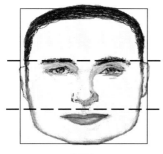
1.26

1.27 Venus ~ Water. Sensitive, flexible, warm, idealistic, caring, creative.
This oval face is typically feminine, with a roundness and softness in all or most features. She has a warm, affectionate, outgoing and upbeat personality. She likes other people, enjoys company and thinks the best of them. Creative by nature she loves her high ideals, has flexibility and creates a very likeable personality. Her outer softness covers an inner strength and good intuition. Romantic and nurturing by nature, her family can take an important space in her life. She can be too trusting at times and can fall victim to those who can readily take advantage of her desire to please others, especially when she has other soft lines.

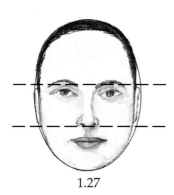
1.27

15

Face to Face with Facts

Basic Structures & Combinations

Common Characteristics of Basic Face Shapes

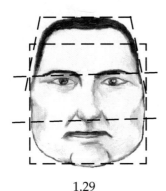

1.28

1.28 Mercury ~ Air. Intellectual, quick, open-minded, organiser, persuasive, restless, needs to be aware of grounding.
The Mercury personality is bright and cheerful. With her high mental and nervous energy, knowledge, status and power are important. She has a talent for teaching and organising others. With her quick wit and persuasive tongue, she loves talking, arguing and meeting people. The wide forehead and pointed chin shows a high mental capacity and lack of grounding. This physical restlessness is matched by the overactive mind, which is endlessly thinking, worrying or absorbing information. Although she is ambitious and enjoys meeting people, she tends to avoid emotional closeness and may have only a few close friends.

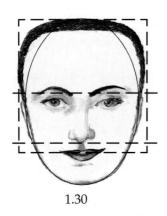

1.29

1.29 Saturn ~ Fire ~ Earth. Volcanic, determined, introverted, earthy passion, intuitive, cautious.
The Saturn personality is easily recognised by the wide, tight jaw, boney, angular structure of the cheekbones, with some depression around the temples and a high but narrow forehead. This structure creates a suppression of the emotions resulting in a sense of loneliness. The strong earthy energy is contained and suppressed psychosomatically, creating an internal fire. He likes to be alone with his thoughts and lacks the warmth and desire to share with others. Instinctively careful and cautious, with an innate shyness, he may find it difficult to find a mate. He may enjoy pondering deep-seated ideas that may be interesting and original.

1.30

1.30 Uranus ~ Water ~ Earth. Strong-minded, compassionate, sensitive, flexible, understanding.
The Uranus personality has a very strong mind, coupled with an understanding, emotional and sensitive nature. The sensitivity and flexibility is a powerful combination that can make her very successful in business and monetary endeavours. The special understanding of people and their needs makes her a *people person*, good at counselling and negotiation. The mental and emotional combination gives her the versatility to relate to a large spectrum of the population. The self-awareness of the high degree of energy of these qualities needs to be delicately balanced for optimum success.

Part 1: The Art of Reading Faces is a Science

Basic Structures & Combinations

Common Characteristics of Basic Face Shapes

1.31 Pluto ~ Water ~ Air. High aspirations, mentally creative, open-minded, emotional sensitivity, needs grounding.
The high emotional sensitivity of the Pluto personality is in a delicate balance with a need for grounding. Her loving and caring nature can be upset when she is not understood by others. Rather than stand her ground, she feels the need to avoid dealing with emotional issues by resorting to reason instead of action. She may find it difficult to verbalise this internal processing. The psychic sensitivity is enhanced by the finer qualities that she constantly aspires to. This can often lead her to altered states of consciousness.

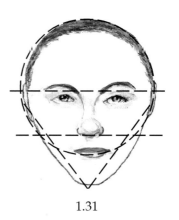
1.31

Case Study

1.32 A Sample Reading at First Glance

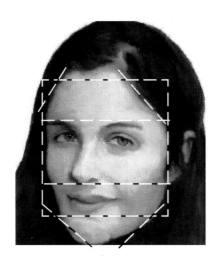

Prominent Feature: Eyes
The squarish middle and lower section with the prominent cheek bones show a strength to achieve her emotional goals in a practical way. She internalises her personal feelings, seen in the tapering hairline and the sensitive chin. The green compassionate eyes show a great inner courage and beauty.

Mars ~ Mercury ~ Saturn
Earth - Air - Fire
(Refer Figures 1.26, 1.28 and 1.29)

17

Face to Face with Facts

Case Study

1.33 Fleshing Out The Framework

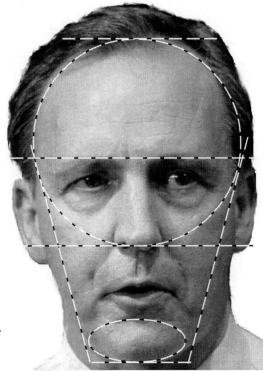

Mental - 48 %
Wide and high
Highly intellectually dominant with a broad and open mind
Over-balances the rest of the personality

Emotional - 26%
Shorter and tapering
Quite controlled and guarded in expressing personal feelings

Physical - 26%
Long but narrowing sharply
Length shows good depth of sensitivity in the business world
But narrowing creates a weaker foundation and grounding.

Very prominent rounded forehead with an excellent memory and creativity. Quick, versatile and inventive

Hooded, careful, deep set and calculating eyes that are narrow, slightly pointed nose Careful and tight with money Expresses feelings sharply

This one will get upset easily when he cannot get what he wants. The full bottom lip says he will freely vocalise his thoughts.

The fleshy protruding chin
One that will push his way to get what he wants

1.34 Sample Reading at First Glance

Idealistic, strong creative mind, warm and emotionally sensitive.

This shows in the rectangular, top two zones with a good balance in each. Bottom triangle shows she needs to stay grounded and watch emotional upsets.

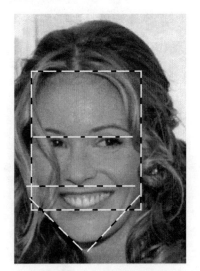

**Jupiter ~ Mercury
Ether ~ Air**
(Refer Figures 1.24 and 1.28)

Part 2

Assessment of the Individual Parts

The Forehead – Frame of the Mind

The Eyebrows – Communication

The Eyes – A Point of View

The Nose – The Personality Knows

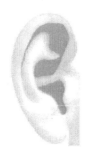

The Ear – Listening Carefully

Assessment of the Individual Parts

The Cheeks and Cheekbones – Ambition

The Lips – The Taste for Life

The Chin and Jaw – Vitality and Foundation

Lines of Development – Tell-Tale Lines

Facial Hair – Grounding and Sensitivity

Part 2: Assessment of the Individual Parts
Facing the World

We **face** the world with the **frontal** area of all the exposed sensory parts of the face. All our five senses and the mind in their full height and width in the three major zones and the individual parts are computing and responding to all the sensory information in front of us. We **project** this sensory equipment into the world in **profile** with the priorities of each zone and the projection of each individual part of sensory equipment according to the unique formation of the profile. This creates in the individual the personality features that show the expression or suppression of their potential characteristics.

When studying the individual parts separately, note:-
* Height, width, and development of the particular part, front view and projection in profile.

* The position of the individual part in the relevant zone, level and balance in comparison to the rest of the face.

This will give you a quick assessment of the quality of expression of that particular feature. (Refer to Figures 1.1 and 1.2 on page 11).

Sample Readings at First Glance

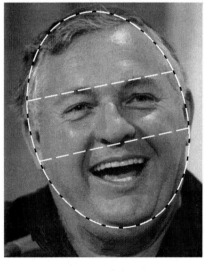

2.1

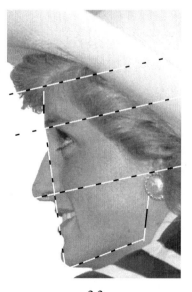

2.2

Emotional, creative and innovative. Note the large area in the emotional and physical show the great love and understanding for money business and the good, earthy things in life. The oval face shows flexibility that can be influenced by earthy desires. The eyes are shrewd and calculating.

The high 75% of energy in the emotional and physical zones show how this person puts into action her desire to understand and help others. The angular jaw shows her determination to fulfill this. The strong, straight nose goes out there to be noticed and do things that are practical.

Face to Face with Facts

The Forehead
The Frame of the Mind

Front View

The exposed area of the forehead that is devoid of hair growth in the frontal area of the head to the eyebrows constitutes the **forehead.** The frame of the mind faces and evaluates the information through **observation** of the **present**, its **memory** of the **past experiences;** and using its **imagination** and **creativity** to decide how it should **respond.**

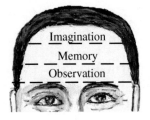

2.3

2.3 The **height** of the forehead shows the degree of intelligence. The **width** (the breadth of view) shows degree of openness, expression and understanding. A narrow or broad-minded person.

2.4 The forehead is further divided into three regions – **observation, memory** and **imagination.** Their development could be wide or closed as seen from the front as it is framed by the hairline. Notice how pronounced or receding it appears in profile.

The section that protrudes the most in profile will be the dominant aspect of mental choice of processing information.

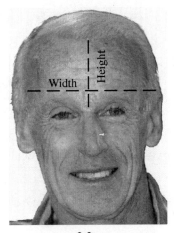

2.3a
Broad and open-minded
High intellect
Good breadth of view

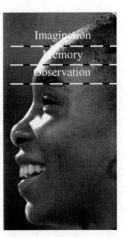

2.4a
Dominant observation
Very open creativity
High intellect, quick mind

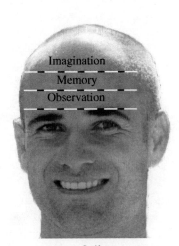

2.4b
Dominant creativity
and imagination
Open-minded

Part 2: Assessment of the Individual Parts

The Forehead
The Frame of the Mind

In Profile

In profile, the **prominence of each zone** of the forehead shows the **preference** the individual uses to process its actions and reactions. It is the priority of how each zone confronts the world and its events that literally creates the unique attitude of the mind of the individual. This is nothing to do with the internal brain function, but the externalisation of information seeking expression and thought forms that create the face construction and shape.

2.5 A high degree of creative imagination that processes information before making a decision.

If the forehead is **straight up,** the person likes and needs detail to make decisions. She is creative, is more imaginative and has a lot on her mind. The further back the hairline receedes it increases the creative capacity of the person. The decisions made have been given a lot of thought. This one could be a bit absent-minded and could need more grounding.

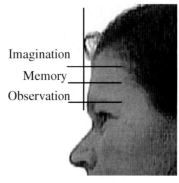

2.5

2.6 An observant intuitive mind, quick to take action.

One with a **sloping forehead** is quicker to make decisions and does not need details because of their quick **mental observations** and **assessment** of the facts. This one could have good intuition and a sense of judgement about people and their feelings. They have a good presence of mind.

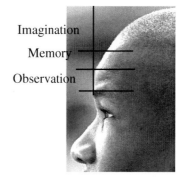

2.6

2.7 A good memory of past events that is calculating and can be analytical.

If the **central dome** is **protruding,** the person has good long-term **memory** recall. This can often result in retaining early conditioning and past experiences. This can be more so if the hair growth is closing in on either side of the forehead in this region.

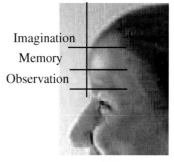

2.7

23

Face to Face with Facts

The Forehead
The Frame of the Mind

The Hairline

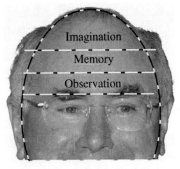
2.8

2.8 The **size** and **shape** of **the frame of the mind** determines how this person pictures the world. The shape formed by the **hairline** and **eyebrows** show how they extend or limit the areas of **observation**, **memory** and **imagination**. Their proportionate distribution then creates the individual personality and their special way of thinking. These proportions are also to be observed in profile to determine their prominence.

2.9

2.9 Straight, Broad and Wide – Broad and **open-minded** this one has a high intellect and an open mind. The straight hairline shows practicality, but the squareness shows a frame of mind that can be limited by unbending steadfastness in her own belief systems.
There is a high degree of creativity and a broad outlook on life.

Note: There is good balance of **imagination**, **memory** and **observation**.

2.10

2.10 Straight, Narrow and Wide – Narrow or **low** hairline but **open-minded**, this person is practical, methodical, likes to get things done rather than think about them. The **rectangular** frame of mind shows that he is steadfast and can be fixed in his way of thinking and may lack creativity or leadership. A good worker that will follow instructions precisely.

Note: **Observation** and **memory** is wide and open while **imagination** is covered and curtailed by a low hairline.

Part 2: Assessment of the Individual Parts

The Forehead
The Frame of the Mind

The Hairline

2.11 Straight, Narrow and Short – *Narrow* but also **closed-minded**, this frame of mind shows that his own mind is still being influenced by his upbringing. The expression of his thoughts may be repressed due to his need to think of others first or seek the need of their approval. This could create a personality that could be typically anxious.

2.11

Note: The **memory** and **imagination** areas are restricted by too much of the past still ringing in his mind. This could restrict his creativity and personal expression. Therefore a major portion of his priorities are focused on emotional or physical needs.

2.12 Broad, Open and Rounded – The **curved** hairline shows a great deal of **flexibility** in thinking. She can be **over-imaginative**, or too open-minded, but has a very creative, intuitive mind with great individuality. She can be gentle and caring and think of others' needs first. The size of the forehead shows a great deal of activity in all areas of thought. This one needs to be constantly aware of being grounded.

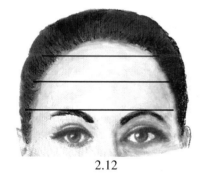

2.12

Note: The height and curve shows flexibility is mostly in the imaginative area, which enhances the creative aspects of both the observation and memory, which are wide and open.

2.13 Peaked – This one's frame of mind shows a **high intelligence** but **narrow view.** What she sees is only her point of view. Closed to other's opinions, she can be vengeful, insecure, or feel inadequate. This single-mindedness is well focused, but lacks the flexibility to accept others due to a restricted imagination.

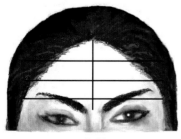

2.13

Note: Wide in observation narrowing down in the memory with only a little area in the imagination section.

Face to Face with Facts

The Forehead
The Frame of the Mind

The Hairline

2.14

2.14 'M' Shaped, the **Widow's Peak** – This free individual likes to be without encumbrances. She can be loving to herself, is artistic, and sensitive. She has the potential for a high intellect, but often doubts herself as the frame of mind indicates a division between the left and right brain.

Note: **Low in the centre** shows her lowered opinion of herself, and **high on either side** indicates the high potential for creativity and imagination. The centre area of memory also closes in, showing that the memories of her past and upbringing restrict her from a open minded expression of her own thoughts. This is what creates the self- doubt. The frame opens out wider again in the observation area.

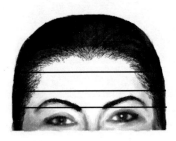

2.15

2.15 Jagged Hairline – This **rebellious frame of mind** is created by the ***unruly hair growth.*** This jagged hairline can be seen as a combination with any of the other frames of mind. It indicates a strong mind that wants an expression of her own and the desire to break through the restrictions placed upon her during her upbringing by society or parenting. This could be an asset when free expression is allowed. Ill-humour and frustration could result until freedom is experienced. She could be at odds with society. When the forehead is high they can make good changes in life.

2.16. Adolf Hitler

2.16 Combination – Note any major differences in the left and right sides. This will indicate a mental (right side) and emotional (left side) conflict or imbalance. For further evidence of this see the comments in the Case Studies of personalities with these imbalances. Refer to the examples, Part 3.5 The Two Faces of Abraham Lincoln and Part 3.9 Alan Bond. Imbalanced Structure. The left and right imbalances or the variation can cause a lot of conflict in the mental attitude of the personality. Note: Case Study on Hitler Part 4.6

Part 2: Assessment of the Individual Parts

The Forehead
The Frame of the Mind
The Hair Length

2.17 (a)

2.17 The Hair acts like antennae reaching out into the energy fields that surround us. They seek out vibrational reactions and transmit them through the skin into sensory tissue in our body. Wherever hairs grow there is an enhancement of sensory awareness to the environment. This relates to hair growth wherever it may be on the face or body.

Length of Hair

2.17 (a) and (b) **Long hair** connects the mind with the emotions as they flow alongside the face and connect with the body. Note how it connects with all three Zones of the face. As it rests on the shoulders it enhances the connection between the head and the body and creates much more grounding and more in contact with matters of the world. The thicker the growth and longer the hair the more grounded and sensitive the person may feel.

2.17 (b)

2.17 (c) **Short hair** or a **shaved** head, is most often seen with men. The cut "*short back and sides*" keeps the mind clear of emotional contact. This heightened mental state is preferred by men in general so they can focus on mental tasks without being clouded by their emotions. This also isolates them from their own feminine aspect and could create less understanding of the women they will need to interact with.

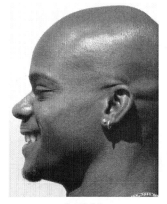

2.17 (c)

The **thickness** and **colour** of the individual hairs will transmit a **higher degree of sensitivity** from very thin and light-coloured hair to the thicker and darker hair quality showing an increasing **degree of vigour, vitality and earthiness** in the stimulation of the owner.

Face to Face with Facts

The Forehead
The Frame of the Mind
The Hair Type

From **sparse** hair to **dense** growth, we will have the stimulation increasing as the denseness increases correspondingly.

Fine hair indicates high sensitive mental vibration, while the coarser or thicker the individual hairs are, the more earthy physical vitality is indicated.

From **straight** to **curly,** the hair has less reaction and holding of the electrical energy when straight. The tighter the curls the harder it will be for the person to resist the external stimulation or let go.

2.18 (a)

2.17 Fringes

To **cover a part** of the forehead indicates a subduing of the open expression of the area covered. This *"buffer zone"* reduces the performance of the qualities that will be challenged. It softens the qualities of the mind, therefore enhancing the emotional sensitivity. With the **forehead clear,** the mental power and a strength of the mind of the same person is enhanced, adding to the openness of the personality. (Refer Figures 2.18 (a) and (b)

Similarly, when the hairline partly covers the left or right side of the face it reduces the expression of the respective side.

2.18 (b)

Note: 2.18 (a) – The lady with the fringe covering the forehead is expressing more of her emotional and physical aspect than the strength of her mind.

In 2.18 (b), the same lady (two years later with the fringe grown out) is now expressing the full mental strength seen in the broad and high forehead. The life expression change has been marked by a fuller expression of her true potential characteristics. This has made her outgoing and has changed her life and her professional outlook.

Part 2: Assessment of the Individual Parts

The Eyebrows
Communication

The Eyebrow Type

2.19 (a) The "eye brows" are the separators between the eyes (*or emotions*) and the brow (*or the mind*). They signify the **degree of understanding** between the **head** and the **heart**. They are the creators or suppressors of expression and **a point of view**. Their movement is controlled by the automatic reflexes of the muscles between the brow and eyes. This helps the person to distinguish the differences between thinking, feeling and action.

The hair growth, thicker in the **centre,** indicates focus and the thinning out at the outer edges indicates an increasing peripheral vision. The thicker, darker and coarser the hair the more earthy, vital and passionate the person. While the finer, lighter or scantier the hair the more sensitive, imaginative with less energy and drive.

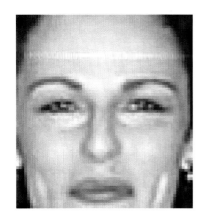

2.19 (a)

2.19 (b) Well-Balanced Eyebrows – When they are moderately spaced apart, a gently curving arch above each eye, with the thickest growth in the beginning gradually thinning towards the edge of the face, they indicate a **balance** of strong energy flow and communication between mind and emotions. When eyebrows grow evenly, sloping along the axis and point away from the midline, they give the person a sense of focus, enthusiasm and apassion for what they set their mind and heart on.

2.19 (b)

2.20 Boomerang-Shaped Eyebrows – These indicate an independence and a strength of will. They like their own way and want to get ahead. These qualities are more pronounced when the angle is sharper. This can be an acuity in observation.

Note: The points reach sharply into the observation area of the mind. This quality has greater precision when this peak is directly over the centre of the iris.

2.20

2.21 Low-Set Eyebrows – This one has a strong mind that suppresses and controls the emotions. His prudent, cool and calculating nature may also have a restricted point of view. The feeling of frowning upon life in general could create stress and tension. This is being physically experienced by the tension required of the muscles of the forehead and the eyes to maintain this expression.

2.21

29

Face to Face with Facts

The Eyebrows Communication

The Eyebrows Set

2.22

2.22 Very High-Set Eyebrows – Shows a *devil may-care-* attitude. This person can be trusting of others or too open-minded, leading to possible disappointments. The openness of emotional expression can make the person feel criticised by others and unable to speak up for themselves. To "*raise your eyebrows in surprise*" is a natural response to the unexpected.

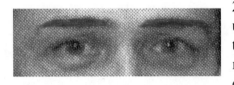

2.23

2.23 Straight Eyebrows indicate a practical, forthright, rather unimaginative person difficult to change views, likes to stick to facts and get on with the job. They have a down-to-earth manner and not easily swayed by their, or other people's, emotions.

2.24

2.24 Eyebrows that are sloping Upwards from Midline show that this person has a high degree of one-pointedness that can be egotistical. This mental point of view could lack emotional warmth and understanding of others' feelings. This one could tend to look down on others and themselves. Their peripheral vision is very open and observant of many things at once. They can be too strong and controlling of their own feelings.

2.25

2.25 When the eyebrows Curve Downwards at the outer edge they tend to protect or reduce the peripheral vision of the person. She could tend to be a bit shy and keep a lot of emotional feelings to herself. This one needs to build more self-confidence as she may find it difficult to get ahead in the world. The nature of this person may be outwardly gentle and soft-spoken, but she may have a bit of frustration of suppressed feelings inside.

Part 2: Assessment of the Individual Parts

The Eyebrows Communication

The Eyebrow Hairs

2.26 Eyebrow Hairs Growing Upwards signify the enthusiasm and passion this person puts into whatever they love to do. As a brave and resolute person, he is ready to accept challenges. The restless energy makes it hard to live a quiet life and he could get bored easily. The coarser and darker the hair the more earthy vitality this one possesses.

2.26

2.27 When Hairs Grow Downward they show a loss of energy and motivation. This person may be mentally or emotionally stressed, or overworked. Since hairs are like antennae their thickness, colour and direction in which they point are good indicators of the quality and vitality of the area they are rooted in. Therefore the thickness and quantity of hair in the eyebrows also shows the degree of separation between the thinking and emotional process and the vitality and forcefulness of expression.

2.27

2.28 Thin or Scanty Eyebrows show lack of energy and direction of purpose. They might find it a challenge to separate their thoughts and feelings. They will demand the attention of others depending on the settings shown above, and the degree of thickness and quantity of hair. The colour, when **light**, shows a tendency towards mental attitudes, while the darker or **blacker** it gets indicates the need for emotional or physical response.

2.28

2.29 Thick, Bushy Eyebrows on the other hand show a vast amount of passion and vitality for what this one sets himself out to do. He can be aggressive by nature due to his enthusiasm. If the hairs grow in different directions the differing thought can create internal conflict in decision making and result in irritability and stress.

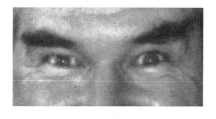

2.29

The Eyebrows Communication

The Eyebrow Position

2.30 Joined Eyebrows show combative, competitive nature. This one can be short-tempered and explosive due to the suppressed internal fire coming up from the solar plexus. The joining of the brow creates a lid on their unexpressed feelings until he literally *"blows his top"*. He can be a high achiever when he learns to open up and allow that pent-up energy to flow the way he knows he can. They want to be winners all the time. This high motivational energy can be a great asset.

2.30

2.31 Sympathetic Eyebrows slope down slightly from the midline and sometimes the ends slope a little more. This person tends to be very understanding and sensitive of others' feelings. This can lead to be being influenced by other people's needs at the expense of her own. The more the outer edges of the eyebrow enfold the outer parameters of the peripheral vision of the eyes the more they will sacrifice their own needs for others. We can say they feel so sorry for others they do not think for themselves. They then learn to bear their own pain quietly. Watch for the muscle activity around the eyes that will indicate the degree of this attitude.

2.31

2.32 Acuity of Vision of both mental and emotional levels are indicated when the **peak of the eyebrow** is directly over the pupil of the eyes. If the peak is closer to the midline this one can be too mentally focused and can be close-minded. The further out this peaking is from the middle of the eye the sharpness of observation is more open-minded. This person is quick to note and react both mentally and emotionally with a broader point of view.

2.32

The **eyebrows** are very clear indicators of the **mental and emotional** reactiveness this person has in their internal relationship within themselves and the **external** world as they observe it. They are powerful **balancers of the Left and Right brain function.**

Note the differences between the left and right eyebrows as shown in the above context.

Part 2: Assessment of the Individual Parts

The Eyes
A Point of View

The Eye Types

2.33 Eyes represent the Heart ~ They are Windows of the Personality and Soul. This is the meeting place of the mind, body and spirit of the human being. It is the most sensitive and reactive part of the person's internal and external reactions. It photographs, internalises and reacts to every moment of human experience.
The rest of the body-mind remembers what the eyes have seen.

In the **Art of Reading Faces,** your Eyes become the photographers of the person you are looking at so you can assess their **personology** in the most sensitive way. They are like sensitive **cameras** that send the vital information to the left and right brain for evaluative reaction and action.

2.33
A Face of Innocence
The Eyes of a Soul

Consider these important factors:–

The **right eye** represents the physical personality, a left brain analytical function. The **left eye** shows the soul potential or right brain and creative functions.

> **Eye set** – Distance apart and depth.
> **Size of eyes** – Large or small
> **Level** of the eyes
> **Balance** of the **eyes**
> **Colour of irises**
> **Quality** of shine, glitter or glaze
> **Pupil** size and **steadiness** of the gaze

2.34

Eye Set

Distance Apart

2.34 When the eyes are set at the distance of one eye-length between the eyes, the person shows a good balance of understanding and evaluation.

2.35 When the eyes are wider apart than one eye-length, there is a lessening of mental quickness, focus and assessment of what is being presented. When too wide, the brain finds it harder to get the hemispheres to act together so the capacity for making decisions lessens.

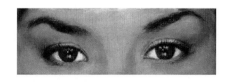

2.35

The Eyes
A Point of View

Eye Set

2.36

2.36 When Set Close together, that is less than a eye-length apart, there is a narrowing of a point of view. Suspicion and lack of warmth results from the person being too self-centred. This creates a feeling of mistrust at times and a sense of loneliness results as he may have only a few friends.

Depth of Eye Set

2.37

2.37 Deep-Set eyes enable this person to be cautious, watchful and observant. He takes time to reflect on what he sees, weighs it up and acts on his own decisions. Emotionally reflective, his feelings are quietly processed internally and expressed with care and often a great deal of compassion and understanding.

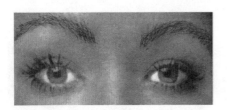

2.38

2.38 Protruding eyes increase the range of vision that can be distracting or unfocused mentally. Emotionally expressive, this one seeks acceptance and appreciation. She is keen to participate in activities and does not like being left out.

Part 2: Assessment of the Individual Parts

The Eyes
A Point of View

Level of Eyes

2.39 Eye levels are distinguished by the horizontal line drawn from the inner to the outer edge of each eye. Eyes should also be level with each other in the face. They define the level of the individual's point of view and balanced perception of the world.
a

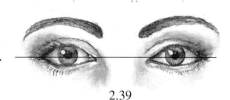

2.39

2.40 When eyes slope upwards from the midline they signify a proud, self-important person who wants to make the most of life. They tend to observe things from a mental point of view and *"look down their noses"* at themselves and others. This critical attitude can motivate them to make the most of life, be energetic and ready to take risks.

2.40

2.41 When eyes slope downwards from the midline they demonstrate a sense of decency, generosity, and a kind nature. They are ready to believe a hard-luck story, have a sensitive heart and like a lasting relationship. They can feel sorry for themselves and others.

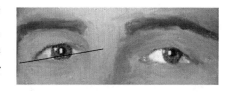

2.41

35

Face to Face with Facts

The Eyes
A Point of View

Size of Eyes

2.42

2.42 Large eyes show a bold, responsible and commanding nature with artistic talents. She is open in the expression of her feelings, is an extrovert with abundant energy and warm enthusiasm of life and all that it brings.

2.43

2.43 Small eyes belong to a cautious and less outgoing person who prefers thinking to doing. She enjoys challenges and prefers working alone. A researcher, analyst or theorist, she can be demanding and loyal. This one may lack some of the energy and exerts more emotional control.

Floating Irises

2.44

The iris should occupy the middle of the open eye with the whites showing on either side only. This will transmit to the brain and the rest of the body-mind a sense of balance, stability and focus between the mental and the physical.

Floating Irises, or **three whites,** is a sign of very high stress with some mental and emotional imbalance.

2.44 When the **whites show below the iris,** this person has lost contact with the physical world. Their eyes roll up showing an unstable, negative character, a danger to himself and others.

2.45

2.45 When the irises sink too low they show the perverse and cruel nature of one that is lonely, unhappy and out of touch with their mind, stuck in their carnal gratification.

Part 2: Assessment of the Individual Parts

The Eyes
A Point of View
Eye Colour

Coloured Glasses

Each person sees the world through the colour of the irises they possess. The colour acts as a vibrational stimulation to the brain's reactions, creating a significant attitude to life as everything they see is affected by the emotional response the colour stimulates in them.

    a) **Brown to Black:** Brown creates a sense of warmth, openness, and passion. This one is an extrovert, excitable and less sensitive to pain. The darker the colour, the deeper the passion and a lessening of warmth and sensitivity. When the irises are black, this person can be so set on the idealistic it could go beyond sensibility.

Warm and Passionate

    b) **Hazel:** Warmth, sensitivity, with greater intellectual vigour. These are the eyes of a kind, warm person that could have a great deal of understanding of others.

Intellectual vigour

    c) **Blue:** From deep sapphire to a washed-out blue. Blue eyes signify a calmer, quieter, more thoughtful person. They are also more conservative and understanding. The lighter the blue, the less passion and compassion. Pale blue eyes can be cool and calculating. Ice-blue eyes have a "*chilling*" look.

Compassionate

    d) **Green:** The '*green fire*' in these eyes signify a courageous, daring, cheerful, clever and inventive person. They have the fire to face the challenges that come their way.

Courage

    e) **Grey:** "*Steely grey*" eyes belong to those who are emotionally controlled and need to think long and hard before committing themselves. They are generally quiet and "*lack-lustre*" as their world does look somewhat grey.

Cold and calculating

    f) **Purple rings** around the iris are noticeable in some eyes that see or aspire towards spiritual concepts or philosophies.

Spiritual and philosophical

Pupil Size

When the **pupils are dialated** they signify some sort of sedated brain function and a loss of focus. The sensitivity of the contraction responses of the iris signifies a somewhat stressed, nervous state that may make them feel "*spaced out*". When the eyelids are opened wider than normal, they will also indicate a high degree of stress.

High stress condition

Face to Face with Facts

The Nose
The Personality Knows

The Size of the Nose

2.46 The Nose protrudes the furthest out of the face and **knows** where you are heading because the rest of the face follows the nose. **It represents your identity**. It is the organ of breath on which your life force and energy intake depends. Its **strength, size** and **proportion** with the rest of the face is an important indication of the projection of one's personality. The nose occupies the space of the Emotional Zone of the face and **bridges** the Mental and Physical Zones. The nose also creates the **centre of balance** and focus as it divides the left and right sides of the face.

2.46

2.47 A well-balanced nose has an equal length to the upper and lower zones, a straight bridge, a rounded fleshy tip, well-shaped flared wings and nostrils that cannot be seen when viewed from the front. This nose signifies qualities of honesty, truthfulness, loyalty, healthy sex drive, an optimistic outlook and a sound view of themselves and their abilities.

2.47

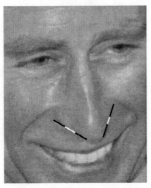

2.48 A Long-nosed person can be a logical planner that takes a long look at things before making a decision. He tends to be snobbish or scornful of others, or have stiffer mannerisms. He tends to **look down his nose** at **lesser** people.

When this **points down** towards the upper lip this one has a high degree of creativity, sensuality and nurturing feelings. It could also indicate a strong sexual desire. The degree of tip tilt and fleshiness accentuates the above characteristics.

2.48

Part 2: Assessment of the Individual Parts

The Nose
The Personality Knows

The Size of the Nose

2.49 Long, narrow nose has some of these attributes of strength and curiosity, but it does not have the width at the base. He is not able to stand up and support his intent. He will often be witty and engaging to cover up this insecurity.

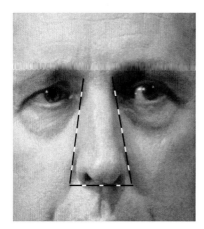

2.49

2.50 A Broad nose is a sign of stability and purpose with better concentration, staying power and success. The width should be concentrated in the lower half of the nose, signifying the determination of the ego to hold his ground.

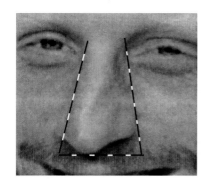

2.50

2.51 A Large nose with a good base belongs to one who will have a great need to project his personality and make a difference in the world where he works. He does especially well in managerial and supervisory jobs where he can show others how good he is and wants others to do the same.

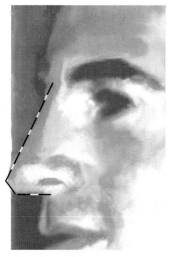

2.51

Face to Face with Facts

The Nose
The Personality Knows
The Size of the Nose

2.52

2.52 A Prominent Arched nose shows she is creative, practical, mentally aggressive and likes to direct others. She likes efficiency, seeks to implement her ideas and likes to see that they are carried out.

2.53 Short noses show less strength and determination to push themselves out there. They show a freer, less responsible or dependable person who enjoys a good time. They have an emotional sensitivity that can feel vulnerable and a lack of personal power.

Self-assertion and personal pride will need to be an important focus to achieve greater freedom in relationships with others.

2.53

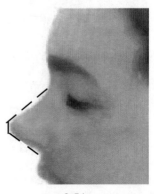

2.54

2.54 A Snub nose turns up at its end so the nostrils are visible. This signifies a happy-go-lucky personality who has difficulty in saving money and making ends meet. I call it a *"ski-jump"* nose, that says to the owner and others *"let us have fun"*. This one can, at times, want to overlook serious challenges or treat them too lightly. Emotionally, she can be a flirt or express sensuality freely if the lips are also full.

Part 2: Assessment of the Individual Parts

The Nose
The Personality Knows
Nose Bridges

Start of the Nose

2.55 When the bone structure **commences straight from the forehead** the personality will have a strong mind expressed more physically and will see things as black and white. The nose divides the face in the emotional zone so the left and right sides do not work together so easily.

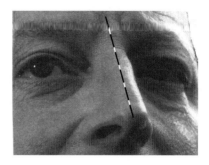

2.55

2.56 When the bone structure **commences between the eyes,** the lower bridge enables both eyes to see the same picture in their peripheral vision. This enables the personality to experience greater emotional balance in issues of the heart. They are softer and have a greater understanding of life.

2.56

Nose Ridge

2.57 When the nose ridge is **slim, prominent** and **arched** it gives the person a high perception of precision and balance. This person likes tidiness, order and is a good organiser, manager and/or accountant.

When the ridge of the nose is **wide and strong**, this person has good strength and stamina but may find it difficult to perceive emotional issues clearly. They can be earthy and physical in handling practical things in life.

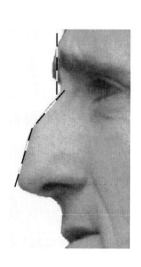

2.57

Face to Face with Facts

The Nose
The Personality Knows
Tip of the Nose

The Tip indicates the attitude of the projection of the person's ego, actions and how it meets the events and people out there.

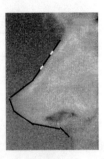
2.58

2.58 A **soft fleshy** tip shows the person is sensitive and projects her actions and speech with a great deal of feelings of consideration, warmth and gentleness. The increase of the fleshiness amplifies these qualities. This one has a good sense for art and beauty.

2.59 A **pointed** tip indicates that she comes to the point or makes her point felt promptly. The sharper the tip and the larger the nose these qualities are increased. This one is also inquisitive and likes to "*poke her nose in other people's business*".

2.59

2.60 A **groove** in the tip shows indecision in making his point or deciding what to do. Work can be emotionally unsatisfying as this one likes to make his point of view stick.

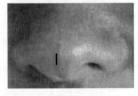
2.60

Shape of the Nostrils

2.61 Flattened wings and narrowed nostrils show poor money sense and find money hard to acquire.

Those with **large nostrils** are financially careless and let money slip through their fingers.

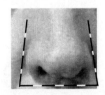
2.61

People with **small** nostrils are careful and steady with money.

2.62 Square nostrils are conservative, thick-skinned and determined. When they are extra **wide** there is a lack of self-control of energy flow. This one can be loose with money.

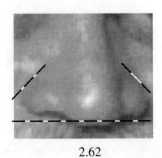
2.62

The nose, whatever its shape and angle, is affected by its fleshiness with good income and skill in business, honesty and dependability. The breathing pattern, vitality and emotional ease is seen in the balance, shape and condition of the nose.

Part 2: Assessment of the Individual Parts

The Ear
Listening Carefully to Reality
Ear Function

The Ear resonates to all frequencies of sound and keeps us in the present. All vibrations are experienced, both **externally** and **internally**. This brings us as close as possible to reality – mentally, emotionally and physically. The ears play a very important role in the analysis of ourselves, or another, as the rest of our senses depend so much on being in touch with the reality of the moment.

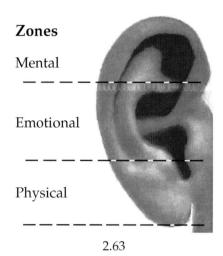

2.63

Note these important points:
  i. The **three zones** on the ear in relation to the three zones on the face;
  ii. The **ridges** and **cups** in each section;
  iii. The **size** of the ear and its development, will affect the importance of the above observation;
  iv. The **setting** of the ear – Its **height** in relation to the three zones of the face; and its **angle** in relation to its own zones;
  v. Always look for any **left** and **right** side **differences**;
  vi. Ear **lobes**.

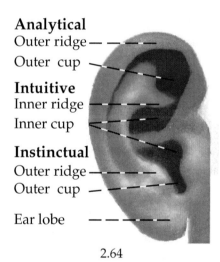

2.64

2.63 The ears listen to reactions pertaining to all three zones of the whole face. Therefore the ear itself can be divided into the upper (or **mental**), the middle (or **emotional**) and the lower (or **physical**) zones.

2.64 The **ridges** separate and create a clarity as the **cup** collects the vibrations at each level.

The **Outer Ridge** and **Cup** collect and respond to **external** sounds. This connects us to the external reality and assists in analytical thinking and actions.

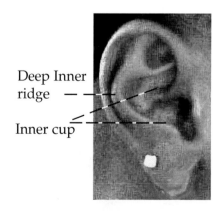

The **Inner Ridge** and **Cup** responds to our inner voice and vibration, which we call intuition. This is the voice of the Soul or psyche. This assists us in our creative thinking and actions.

2.65 Intuitive ear with a deep inner ridge and cup.

2.65

43

Face to Face with Facts

The Ear
Listening Carefully to Reality
Ear Size

2.66

2.66 Large ears connect to all three Zones. They extend into the mental or physical, or both zones. This one is highly sensory to sound and more anchored to the present, mentally and physically. He is kind, receptive and generous to others, expressing his feelings with actions. This one's ear is a little lower, showing there is a lot of emotional and practical application to living in the present.

2.67

2.67 Medium-sized ears connect to the mental and physical zones being approximately one-third of the three zones of the face. This will give a good balanced reaction of all three aspects of the personality. This one is emotionally steady, calculating and has great endurance in achieving his goals.

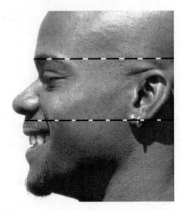

2.68

2.68 Small ears respond more to personal needs and trust one's self more than others. He is not a good listener. The ear itself could be tight due to the strain of wanting to hear clearly or restrain expressing reactions. This one may need to be more present and grounded.

Part 2: Assessment of the Individual Parts

The Ear
Listening Carefully to Reality

Ear Settings

Height in relation to the Zones on the face

2.69 When the **top of the ears** are touching or slightly above the line of the Mental Zone line, they show sufficient mental contact. As they cover the whole emotional zone they have good contact with the feelings. The bottom of the ear where it is still attached to the face should connect at the line at the physical zone or lower to give sufficient expression of this one's reaction in the physical reality of life. This one shows a good balance of all three zones. She is mentally very alert and quick, warm, affectionate and dependable and has good expression of her physical capabilities.

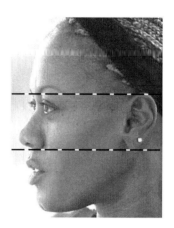

2.69

2.70 When they are **set low** and part of the ear is in the physical zone, this enables the person to be more compassionate, understanding and willing to help others who need physical and emotional assistance. They have great physical vitality and endurance and are persons of action and feelings.

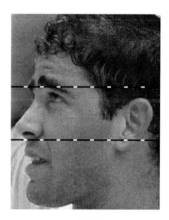

2.70

2.71 Ears that are **high set** connect to the mental and emotional zones so this one tends to be more analytical, precise and imaginative. They show less compassion so can stay more assertive of their own needs and feelings. They often listen and stick to their own point of view. They are often good administrators and control others without their emotions being affected.

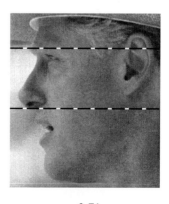

2.71

Face to Face with Facts

The Ear
Listening Carefully to Reality

Ear Settings

2.72 When the ears are **set far back towards the back of the head,** there is a greater projection of the whole personality and this supports a greater intellectual vigour. This one wants to push himself out into the world to express all he has.

2.72

2.73 When the **ears stick out** from the head, they indicate a testing or traumatic upbringing. This one is a rebel that wants to create change. They can be great leaders with strength and balance in other features.

Ears that are **close** and **flat to the head** show that this person will agree and conform to standards set. As the saying goes *"we get our ears pinned back"* or *"put in our place"*. This understanding of what others want, and how to conform, could be a valuable marketing asset.

2.73

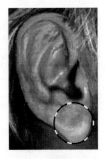

2.74

Ear Lobes

Ear lobes are the fleshy part at the bottom of the ear that hang free below the attached part of the ear. They are in the physical zone of the face, and show by their size and fleshiness the amount of mental, spiritual and emotional expression one is expressing through actions in the physical world.

2.74 **Large long lobes** that hang free indicate a spiritually and emotionally sensitive person with a great understanding of personal needs. This is expressed by his attitude and way of life.

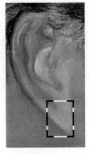

2.75

2.75 When the ear is attached **without any ear lobe,** this indicates an emotionally controlled type. Personal needs are important to this one and his higher ideals are not shared freely by his physical actions.

46

Part 2: Assessment of the Individual Parts

Cheeks and Cheekbones
Ambition/Cheekiness

Types of Cheekbones

The cheekbones give support, character, strength and a sense of power to the emotional aspect of the person. The support and prominence they bring to the area around the eyes, nose and width of the face enhances the qualities of the ego, personal identity and the love and compassion of the heart that expresses the creativity of the individual.

2.76 Cheekbones that are bony and highly visible and protrude outside the vertical face line show the potential this one has to use their inner purpose and achieve their ambition with a single-mindedness in spite of the challenges they might face. Softness and emotional sensitivity will not stop them from getting what they want.

2.76

2.77 High cheekbones that are **well covered** and **fleshy** show a power of command. This person will attain authority with a sense of understanding and emotional sensitivity. These qualities will be enhanced by the degree of fleshiness.

2.77

2.78 High flat cheekbones suggest a high sense of personal dignity. This one can achieve a high position in life in fields that she sets her heart on. She will be successful in the fields of fine arts, academic expression and literature.

2.78

Cheeks and Cheekbones
Ambition / Cheekiness

Types of Cheeks

The Cheeks

Fleshy cheeks are the containers of emotional expression. It is the fleshiest and softest part of the face that registers sensitivity, warmth, health and the reserves of vitality. The fleshiness personifies a cheekiness experienced by humour, fun and wit. They bring joy and fun with a caring and nurturing attitude.

2.79

2.79 Full, chubby cheeks show the affectionate and nurturing nature of the person. He would like to please people and see that they are happy and well looked after. He can tend to give to others more than to himself.

2.80

2.80 When **cheeks are lean** the sense of feelings for the self and others diminish. The lessening of emotional responsiveness could enhance the mental attitude so that this one deals with emotional issues in a reasoning and somewhat unfeeling way.

Part 2: Assessment of the Individual Parts

The Mouth and Lips
A Taste for Life

Types of Mouths

The mouth is the organ of taste and the shape and structure of the lips clearly show the person's taste for life. Life can be **sweet, sour, bitter, spicy** or **astringent.** If you were to put food of each of these tastes in your mouth, the lips would automatically react to each of these tastes.

The mouth is the most mobile part of the face. The muscles and tissue are the softest and most vibrant. The mouth represents the genital organs, or the creativity, of the individual. The lips **speak, feel, express** or **suppress thoughts, emotions** and **sexuality.** The ideal mouth should be moderate in size, full and well shaped. Each lip should be of equal thickness, firm, soft and fit well together. This signifies a warm, honest, caring yet open nature, with a strong character and purpose.

2.81

2.81 The **top lip,** and its **fullness,** shows the degree of sexuality and sensuality – *"Hot lips"*.

The **bottom lip** shows the freedom of vocal expression – *"Tight-lipped"*.

2.82

2.82 A large mouth is mobile, openly expressive and belongs to one who is outgoing, an extrovert, and generous. She attracts attention and popularity. She may have a weakness of resolve or speak too loosely. There could also be a lack of warmth or sexual passion.

2.83 The person with a **small mouth** has her lips pursed to speak but has learnt to hold back the words. She could be a bit introverted, careful and cautious. There also may be a lack of confidence. This could lead to her being suspicious and avoid company or spending money.

2.83

Face to Face with Facts

The Mouth and Lips
A Taste for Life
Types of Lips

2.84

2.84 Thin lips lack warmth and genuine sympathy for others, so it is possible he may have an inferiority complex. Life has turned bitter for him for he has few close relationships, can be lonely, unbalanced and insensitive by nature. He can be hard and tight-lipped with a lot of suppressed grief. Note the degree of thinness.

2.85

2.85 Lips in a **straight line** belong to those who are careful and calculating. They have an orderly mind that interferes with their emotional responses. When this straight line is uneven, there is a tendency to be uptight, impulsive, troubled and misunderstood. This one can be very sensitive but protective about showing their feelings.

2.86

2.86 Lips with an even, **upward curving line** at the corners of the mouth indicate a persuasive, outgoing, creative person with close family ties and wealth. This person has a constant internally smiling nature and expresses her creativity and artistic talents. Sensual by nature, there is a good level of sex drive.

Part 2: Assessment of the Individual Parts

The Mouth and Lips
A Taste for Life
Types of Lips

2.87 The point of sensitivity, when prominent on the top lip, is a indication of a high degree of sensual and sexual sensitivity. The lips are like the labia of the female genitals and the sensual tip is likened to the clitoris. The fullness of this point, when supported by a full top lip, can be obvious in highly sensual people.

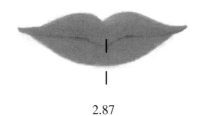

2.87

2.88 The point of refinement is seen on the top lip where it is created by the bow, giving a fullness and even shape. This indicates a high degree of intuitive and nurturing capacity. This one can also be academically eminent, creative and artistic.

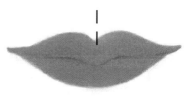

2.88

2.89 Sensuous or sexual lips are noted by the fullness, especially when the upper lip protrudes over the lower lip. This one can be over-nurturing, over-keen to please others, affectionate and with a lot of passion.

2.89

2.90 When the **lower lip protrudes,** it shows this person will talk freely expressing her thoughts and emotions and can "*give plenty of lip*" if she gets upset.
When the **upper lip protrudes** more than the lower it shows the degree of sensuality of the person.

2.90

Face to Face with Facts

The Jaw
The Foundation of Life
Types of Jaws

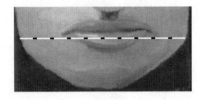

2.91

2.91 A Wide jaw shows great strength and energy of will. This may be so by sacrificing emotional needs dominated by a strong mind. The jaw will then show a lot of tension. This wide jaw shows a determination to support whatever one puts his mind and heart to do and the vitality to carry it out.

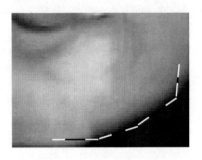

2.92

2.92 A Deep jaw, when viewed from the side, also shows great strength of will, a resolute and determined nature with an ability to achieve, in spite of difficult challenges. The depth of the jawbone shows how deeply one lays the foundations for what they plan to do.

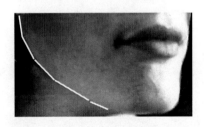

2.93

2.93 A Curved jawbone shows a flexible person that can be swayed by others. She sometimes lacks direction as she may not feel supported in her efforts. This one can be academically a high achiever, but needs grounding to be successful.

Part 2: Assessment of the Individual Parts

The Chin
The Support of Life
Types of Chins

The strength of the jaw and chin give the characteristics of the personality foundation and grounding. The chin signifies the willpower, need for love, security and good health late into life. The chin should be broad, deep and full, showing generosity, physical strength and emotional warmth.

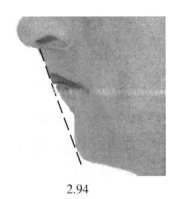
2.94

2.94 Weak receding chin is sloping back from the base of the nose and does support his personal identity. He might find it difficult to stick to his intention when challenged or speak up for himself.

2.95 The person with a **chin jutting** forward shows an extra sense of determination, often to her own detriment, or of others. The strong mental drive forward could often jeopardise her own emotional security. A *stick your neck out* attitude.

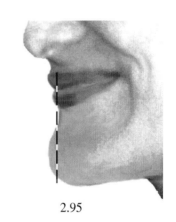
2.95

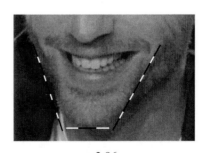

2.96 A pointed chin shows a very sensitive person that can get easily upset. This one needs to be aware of the need to stay grounded. Often this part of the face lacks sufficient vitality.

2.96

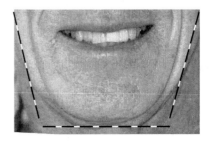

2.97 A wide chin shows a very strong and stable person that will stand fast and carry through whatever project he is set on doing. This one can be quite grounded and has great physical vitality. This one can be quite financially successful.

2.97

Face to Face with Facts

The Lines of Development
The Tell-Tale Lines

Thinking Lines

Lines develop in a face over a period of time as the muscles move repeatedly in a consistent fashion. By habitual reaction in the tissue lines are created by the attitude of the person, leaving its marks of the unique characteristics of the personality. These line develop significantly on the **forehead**, between the **eyebrows**, corner of the **eyes** and as **cheek lines.**

2.98 a

2.98 Forehead Lines – Thinking Lines
These lines are created by the habitual raising of the eyebrows. The are called **inspiration lines,** adding bright ideas to what you already know. A forehead without creases lacks character. Each line represents the characteristics, or quality, named symbolically after an astrological sign. When there are more than four they can create an overload of inspiration. They are positive when they are long, unbroken and dip a little in the middle. **Three lines are the best balance.**

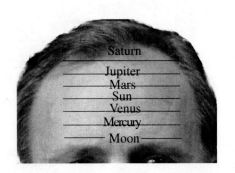

2.98 b

Read lines from **eyebrows** (bottom) to **hairline** (top):

* **Moon:** Good intuition and artistic sensitivity, love of the sea.
* **Mercury:** Quick thought process and verbal fluency and writing.
* **Venus:** Love of physical pleasure and comforts, musical talents.
* **Sun :** Personal pride, dignified manner and carriage, desire for power, prestige and respect for law and order.
* **Mars :** Motivation, aggressiveness, has good energy, courage and stamina.
* **Jupiter:** Love of knowledge, personal pride, wealth and dignity
* **Saturn:** Mediator, philosopher and creative thinking religious knowledge

Part 2: Assessment of the Individual Parts

The Lines of Development
The Tell-Tale Lines

Lines of Focus and Concentration

The physical reaction to metal focus is seen in the pulling together of the muscles of the **eye** and **brow**. This is the external reaction of the brain's attempt to get the right and left hemispheres to work together to achieve a balanced decision. This repeated muscular contraction leaves tell-tale lines between the eyebrows. These lines, when well formed, are rising towards higher aspirations, climbing closer to the forehead line of The Sun (or ambition). Each line, or combination of lines, tells their own story.

2.99

2.99 **A single upright vertical** line between the eyebrows has been developed by this person's determination and single-mindedness. This one can be dogmatic. He may attain a high position in life through his own efforts.

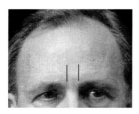

2.100

2.100 **Two parallel vertical lines** between the brows shows that this one is more balanced using both left and right brain, especially if the lines are equal. He will be successful, will rise to power, keep his friends and be respected.

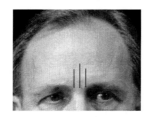

2.101

2.101 **Three vertical lines** show the combined strength of 2.99 and 2.100 (above). This person has the powerful mental focus and a sense of balance that will take him through to achieve whatever he sets his sights on. This one has indeed unusual qualities when the other parts of the face are also supportive of these talents.

2.102

2.102 When the **lines slope inwards** this one may feel indecisive and confused by his internal self-judgement. Thoughts seem to be at cross-purposes. This one needs to come into the physical and practical issues of life that will create more grounding in his life.

2.103 When one or both **bend,** they indicate a lack of support created by some self-doubt and loss of identity.

2.103

55

Face to Face with Facts

The Lines of Development
The Tell-Tale Lines

Crow's Feet

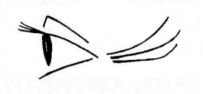

2.104

2.104 Lines at the **outside corner** of the eyes that are **curving upward** show a uplifting or happy outlook on life. This is a demonstration of achievement and a strong mental focus, creating a slight narrowing of the eyes for greater mental clarity.

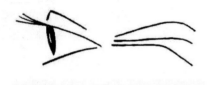

2.105

2.105 When the lines **curve downward,** the emotional and physical reaction of being put down by life in general. This outlook on life could result in continuing unfortunate reactions at work or home.

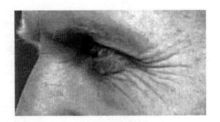

2.105 and 2.106

2.106 **Crossing lines** are created by analysis and being at cross-purposes with an event in life. This could create frustration or confusion caused by conflicting obvservations.

2.106

Part 2: Assessment of the Individual Parts

The Lines of Development
The Tell-Tale Lines

Cheek Lines

2.107 **Cheek lines** that commence on the sides of the nose, readily formed by a smile and extend towards the chin, show an open and creative personality. When the lines are long and even, they indicate a combination of the identity (nose), creativity (mouth), and action (chin). As these three work together with strength and balance, this person can be quite successful in life.

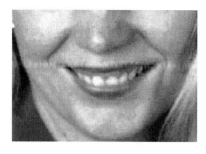
2.107

2.108 When **these two** are supported by lines coming down from the **corners** of the **mouth** it shows great success and attainment of a high position in business, art or literature.

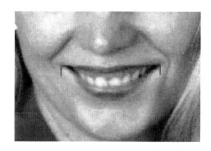
2.108

2.109 When these (refer 2.108 and 2.109) are joined by a **second set of cheek lines** they indicate great wealth, high position and long life. This one has a lot to smile about. He is expressing great creativity, established personal identity and with these, supported by a lot of effort put into it (from cheeks to chin), has become very successful.

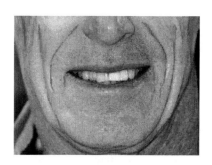
2.109

2.110 Mandarin (curve outward) – This one achieves a high position but without much authority in business. The openness of creative expression freely given shows in the spreading of the descending lines from the nose flowing outwards at the mouth level, demonstrating the nurturing and caring quality of the cheeks.

Shorter lines that swing sharply down show a loss of energy and creativity or vital life force, depending on where the lines fall away.

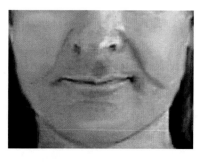
2.110

57

Facial Hair
Vitality and Sensitivity
Hair on the Face

2.111

2.111 **Hairs** act as antennae, drawing vibrations from the outside into the skin and passing some of its own reactions out. They therefore **enhance sensory awareness** wherever they are growing on the face or body. When sensory awareness diminishes with age, hair growth may **increase** in the emotional and physical areas of the face and body. This is to sustain necessary **sensitivity** in these areas. **Hair loss** is incurred in the mental areas when the thinking is increasingly internalised. One may notice an increase of hair growth in the ears, nose, sideburns, moustaches and beards. As the physical vitality diminishes even further, there may be further hair loss, even in these areas.

Moustache

The moustache stimulates and connects the sensuality and creativity from the upper lip to the nose, giving identity and expression. The word **moustache** describes the stashed energy of the mouth (creativity) and nose (ego or identity) combined and whether it is expressed or suppressed according to how it is "*worn*".

2.112

2.112 **Short and squat –** This moustache is kept short and contained directly under the nose and covering the top lip. This encentuates the ego that is self-centred and contained. This enhances the need for control as seen in this typical "Adolf Hitler'" moustache.

2.113

2.113 **Open and reaching outwards –** The flow of energy starts from the base of the nose spreading outwards with the upper lip expressing the creativity openly. The gentle downwards slope signifies the grounding and application of this one's feelings.

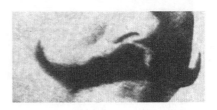

2.114

2.114 **Reaching outwards with tips pointed and up –** This one reaches out, but with the tips pointed up, he is indicating the high self-esteem and opinion he claims as his birthright. It "*points*" to the higher aspiration of personal identity and a position in life.

Part 2: Assessment of the Individual Parts

Facial Hair
Vitality and Sensitivity
Sideburns and Beards

Sideburns

2.114a **Sideburns** are grown by those who feel a need to connect their thoughts to more emotional and physical needs and issues. They are often used to join the hair of the head and the beard on the chin and jaw to feel a sense of grounding in life. The fathers of the nation, religious leaders and those "wise men" that sat in judgement sported beards and sideburns that they *stroked thoughtfully*.

Beards

2.114 a) and b)

2.114b **Full Beards** enhance the energy around the jaw and chin, enabling the person to be more grounded and down to earth in their way of life. It helps to anchor the consciousness in the physical events of life. When it is clear around the lips and cheeks it provides an openness of actions, affections and expression. When it is too bushy and clutters the cheeks and lower lip, the above emotional attributes are internalised, creating some frustration.

2.115 **Pointed or tailored beards** – When the beard is separated from the emotional and mental areas, it creates a greater focus on physical implementation of ideas with less emotional involvement.

Hair growth on the chin signifies or adds to the vitality of that area. When growth is sparse, there is a loss of vitality or grounding. If hair growth is heavy or coarse, the opposite extreme is indicated. When hair is curly it holds on to the energy, so as it gets from wavy to straight there is a smoother flow of awareness and stimulation in that area.

2.115

Part 3

Identification of Potentialities
The Science of Energy Flow and Sacred Geometry

Intellectual ~ Financial ~ Physical

Reliability and Determination

Projection of the Personality

Creativity, Memory and Intuition

Self-Control and Spontaneity

Love and Sensuality

Health, Vitality and Longevity

Happiness and Emotional Stability

Case Studies of
Notable Personalities

Part 3:
Identification of Potential Characteristics

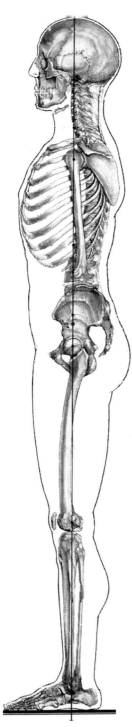

3. 1. Structure = Balance

The Science of Energy Flow and Sacred Geometry

Structure and Balance

3.1 Skeletal Structure = Geometric Energy Flow

Structure directs the **Geo-Metric** flow of energy. **Structure** holds this direction for consistency of performance. This is how we direct **Energy** to fulfil a particular purpose. When the structure is in **balance** the tasks are performed with greater efficiency. This basic principle applies to life itself and all functions of life on earth.

These principles can be seen in the Structure and Balance of a house, a motor vehicle, construction equipment, town planning, a Japanese garden, the lay of the land, the mountains and the movement of the sea. Trees, birds, animals and humans all have specific structure for performing their required roles in life. This sacred geometry of energy flow is recognised by our own experience of this energy within us. We are all those things out there and also inside here as we share the one Universal Intelligence of the Creator. This sacred knowing is our own secret, often unconscious until we make a conscious effort to be aware of what have in us. Our **skeletal structure** is the most complex geometric structure on earth that measures balance and performance throughout all the muscles, tissue, organs and their organised systems of function.

The human "Genome" is frantically busy encoding and decoding biochemical responses in the cellular **structure** to restore function and **balance**. Science is only just experiencing a glimpse of creation. We can now watch 3 billion biochemical "*letters*" spell out our tens of thousands of genes. These genes, strung out along the 46 chromosomes, in virtually every human cell, carry instructions for making all tissue, organs, hormones and enzymes in our body. We translate this information into performance from cellular to behavioural level as emotions: **e-motions** – energy in motion.

Face to Face with Facts

Identification of Potential Characteristics
The Science of Energy Flow and Sacred Geometry
3.2 Structure and Balance.
Compare right ~ left in all areas

Right side of face = Left Brain | **Left side of face = Right Brain**

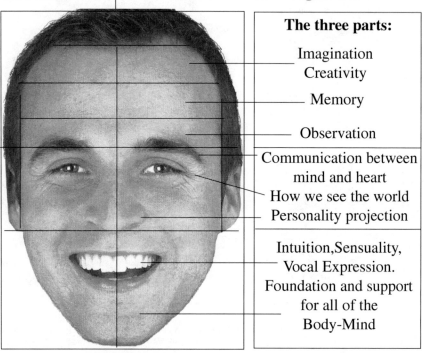

The Three Zones
1. Mental Zone
Frame of Mind
Mental attitude to life
Exposed portion of the Forehead
Frontal and Profile

2. The Emotional Zone
Eyebrows
Eyes
Nose

3. The Physical Zone
Lips and Mouth
Chin and Jaw
Facial hair

The three parts:
Imagination
Creativity
Memory
Observation
Communication between mind and heart
How we see the world
Personality projection
Intuition, Sensuality, Vocal Expression.
Foundation and support for all of the Body-Mind

3.2 Potential Characteristics

Everything that the body-mind is facing in life is seen in the face. We come "**Face to Face with Facts**" as the five senses are represented in the face and the unique balance and structure of each face gives the detailed impressions it receives and transmits.

Part 1 and **Part 2** of this book teaches you the Art of Reading the Face using all these principles. **Part 3** is focused on identifying particular characteristics that indicate the **potential** of **each personality**. This will give you greater insight, at a glance, who and what you are dealing with. This places you many steps ahead in decision making, creating confidence and getting what you want.

It is important to note what characteristics are **prominent.** They are the ones that will dominate or override the ones that are less significant. Stay away from minor details. Study the face from as many angles as possible; **Face to Face and in Profile.**

The **projection** of facial structure shows the force of those attributes.

Part 3 Identification of Potentialities

The Science of Energy Flow and Sacred Geometry
Structure and Balance = Potential for Performance
Part 1 and Part 2 ~ Summary

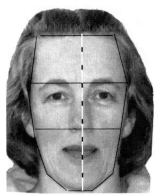

3.3 Front ~ Face Value

a) Face shape: Rectangular - Oval
b) Good Balance in all three Zones
c) Height - good Capacity - balanced
d) Width - good Expression - adaptability
e) Right - Mental - Personality 55%
f) Left - Emotional - Soul 45%
g) Prominent forehead strong mind
h) Slight emotional holding back.

3.3 The Face in Front View ~ *Face value*

a. **Facing** the world: Overall **Face shape**
b. **The three zones: Mental - Emotional - Physical**
c. **Height** shows **Capacity** in each Zone; compare each zone.
d. **Width** shows the degree of **expression** and **action**.
e. **Right half** of the face expresses the **personality – left brain.**
f. **Left half** of the face shows the **soul** or creativity – **right brain.**
g. Any individual **prominent** part of the face.
h. Any **individual part** noticeably restrained – suppressed.

3.4 The Face in Profile ~ *Depth of value*

a. **Projecting** energy forward to meet the world.
b. The distance of **projection** from the **ear** to **nose tip**.
c. **Proportion** of the three **Zones**.
d. The most **outstanding** feature.
e. The **zone** that projects more than the others.
f. The **individual part** that **projects** prominently.
g. The individual parts that **recess** noticeably.
h. The **ear slope**, its **size** and the **zones** it occupies.

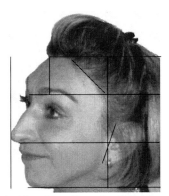

3.4 Profile ~ Depth of Value

a) Projects everything she has got!
b) Highest projection personality love.
c) Emotional - 45% Physical - 30% Mental - 25%
d) Eyes - Warm, loving, open-hearted
e) Emotional zone - very loving, outgoing and willing to push herself forward
f) Nose - curiosity, outgoing personality
g) Sloping forehead - quick intuitive mind

Face to Face with Facts

The Science of Energy Flow and Sacred Geometry
Structure and Balance = Potential for Performance

Right ~ Left side comparisons show the degree of **Mental-Emotional** Balance and their differences in the three Zones

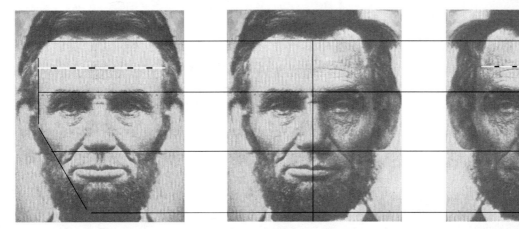

Two Rights Sides   Actual Face   Two Left Sides

3.5 Case Study: The Two Faces of Abraham Lincoln
High degree of Mental-Emotional Conflict

Right - Left Brain - Mental - Analytical - **Personality**	**Left** - Right Brain - Emotional - Creative - **Soul**
Mental - Open-minded - High aspirations, spoke his **mind**	**Emotional** - Closed-minded internalising **feelings**
Deep-set eyes some caution in self-expression – pain	**'M'** shaped **hairline** - Emotional **self-doubt:** imaginative
Tight top lip with corner turned down; bitter and cynical	**Guarded** emotional pain suppressed for a long time
Full bottom lip good vocal expression of thoughts	**Tight top lip** suppressed sexuality and creativity
Cheek to **chin**, sharp tapering: quite low physical vitality	**Smaller mouth** tight lipped about personal emotions
	Wider at the **jawline** shows a determination to succeed
Cheeks show a **drained** emotional and physical energy	**Hollows** under **eyes - cheeks:** low emotional response

The high degree of left and right differences shows that Abraham Lincoln lived through a great deal of mental-emotional conflict. Coming from a restricted and closed-minded upbringing where emotions were taught to be suppressed and ideological beliefs were strong he reasoned with an open mind that brought him a lot of emotional strife (note forehead width – height and "M" shaped hairline).
The prominent cheekbones devoid of much fleshiness shows an ambition to achieve "*no matter wha*t". The wide left jaw shows he gritted his teeth to suppress the emotional pain that he faced, even though sensitive issues in the physical world upset him; (see the pointed chin) in the two right sides.
The lips show that life was a bitter struggle yet he spoke up and fought for his ideals. The large outstanding ears indicate he was very alert to a lot of challenges around him. The emotional darkness that surrounded and haunted him left him a lonely man with very great challenges in life.

Part 3 Identification of Potentialities

Structure and Balance = Potential for Performance

Imbalanced Structure and Proportions create Imbalances of Performance of Potential Characteristics

3.6 Case Study: The Potential for Performance

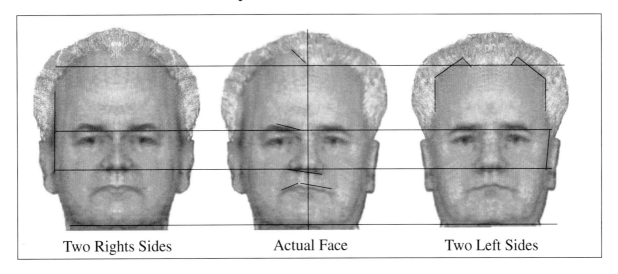

Two Rights Sides — Actual Face — Two Left Sides

3.6 Slobodan Milosevic

a) **Face shape: Square:** Solid, unmoved, practical, earthy, hard working.

b) **Height** and **width** almost equal; he gives it all he has got.

c) **The Three Zones;** Mental **50%** - Emotional **24%** - Physical **26%**
The very High Mental dominance leaves little room for emotional and physical sensitivity and peoples' personal needs. The Mental ideology must be achieved at all costs! **Note: The imbalanced "*Frame of Mind*"** – Right ~ Left

d) **Right-Mental** – Personality **60%**. The very strong dominance of the mind shows in the muscular compression of the right side in the emotional and physical sections. This is indicated by the eyebrow angle, lifted nostril and pulled down corner of the tight mouth all on the right side.

e) **Left-Emotional** – Soul **40%**. This shows a good balance except the tight jaw and lips due to the mental control over all his feelings. The "*M*" shape frame in the left hairline shows how the left is divided against the right by the mental conflict. The small tight eyes show the hidden and suppressed pain that at times may make him shut off feelings and compassion. The Domed forehead in the memory area (middle) shows he never forgets, coupled with the very wide protruding chin shows a stubbornness that will also not forgive if anyone crosses his path. His mind when made up cannot be shifted.

Face to Face with Facts

Structure and Balance = Potential for Performance

The Intellectual and Strong Minded ~ The Outstanding Forehead

Principal Indicators (Ref. Forehead and Hairline Part 2)

3.7a) Hi-tech Fighter-pilot trainer

a) **Prominence** of **Forehead** ~ front and profile
b) **Frame** of **Forehead** ~ Broad and open-minded
c) **Balance** and flow between **Left** and **Right**
d) Note the **dominance** of the three **Mental Sections**:-
 Observation - Memory - Imagination and Creativity.
e) Substantial **support of** the **Mental Zone** by either the Emotional or Physical, or both for its performance.

3.7 Hi-tech fighter-pilot trainer

a) Very high capacity for quick creative thinking ~ highly developed memory and creative domes.
b) Frame of Forehead ~ Broad and open-minded
c) Good balance and flow between Left and Right
d) Note the dominance of the Mental Zone:-
 Good memory - imagination and high degree of creativity.
e) Substantial support of the Mental Zone by the Emotional, very sensitive and delicate pointed chin - must stay centred.

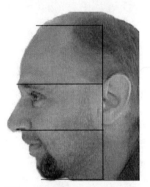

3.7a) Hi-tech fighter-pilot trainer

3.8 Albert Einstein ~ Intellectual of the century

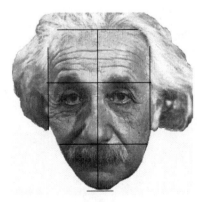

3.8 Albert Einstein

a) Mental **40%** Emotional **40%** Physical **20%**
 Mental and emotional dominance.
b) **Good Left ~ Right balance:** Personality ~ Soul
c) **Forehead** good **height** and **width:** very broad and open-minded.
d) Prominent **projection** of forehead in profile.
e) Forehead overhangs the eyes that are very deep set.
f) **Development lines** on the forehead
 Intuition lines good ~ Moon
 Communication line a little faint and broken ~ Mercury
 Warmth, love for his work strong, right across ~ Venus
 Ambition line runs right across clearly ~ Apollo
g) **Large nose** - Fleshy tip indicate enterprising curious to learn with sensitivity and affection

Part 3 Identification of Potentialities

Structure and Balance = Potential for Performance
Financial and Administrative Success
Principal Indicators:

a) A major portion of the face should occupy the **two lower Zones:** Emotional and Physical: success is needed on earth.
b) **Good width** in both areas gives good expression, adaptability and support. Physical vitality and conscious enthusiasm are experienced and expressed here.
c) **Balance** and flow between **Left and Right** is necessary for sound judgement.
d) A **prominent Nose** indicates the capacity to *"be out there"*.
e) A **strong Jaw** gives the determination to be self-supporting.
f) **Full Lips** show creativity and sensuous appetite for success.

Case Study : 3.9 Alan Bond: Imbalance Structure = Imbalance Performance

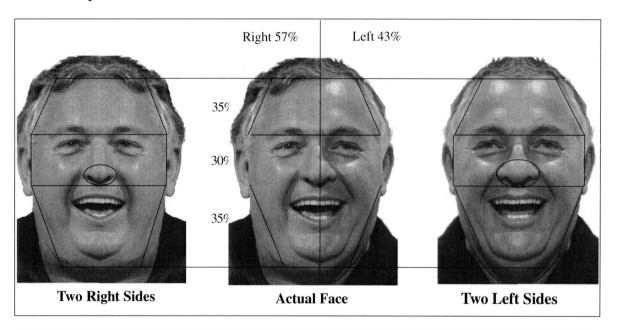

Two Right Sides — **Actual Face** — **Two Left Sides**

Alan Bond's overall face shape is oval with some excess fleshieness in the physical zone depicting a sensitive and flexible personality attached to excesses in physical needs seen in the double chin and jaws. The outstanding structural differences in the left and right sides of the personality is very noticeable in the hairline, nose and chin, this shows conflict between the analytical and creative aspects of himself. As the nose represents money issues, trustworthiness, dependability, the nostrils and tip of Alan's nose shows a great imbalance in dealing with these issues in life. The **two right** sides show the openness of the frame of mind and well-balanced nose. The **two left** sides show a closed frame of mind and the nose of a person who likes to gamble with money and not in balance in his dealings with others. The wide and double chin on the left shows a determination to get what he desires, while the right shows the chin as softer and sensitive. The eyes are shrewd and watchful that guards a lot of his inner feelings often covered by his outward affable laugh and good vocal expression of his creativity, a taste for excesses of life with a warm, caring person under it all.

Structure and Balance = Potential for Performance

Case Studies: Financial and Administrative Success

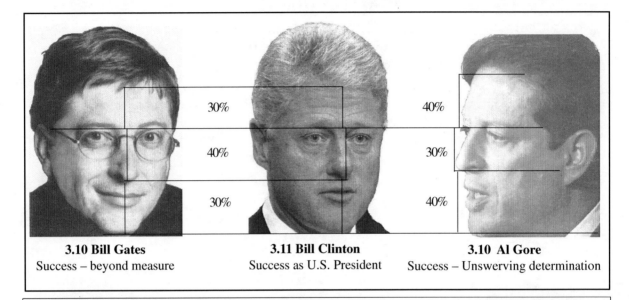

3.10 Bill Gates
Success – beyond measure

3.11 Bill Clinton
Success as U.S. President

3.10 Al Gore
Success – Unswerving determination

3.10 Bill Gates and 3.11 Bill Clinton They both show a major portion of their faces in the two lower zones. With good width in the emotional zone they have the adaptability and understanding to deal with peoples' needs. This is one of the most important criteria for success in daily life. Gates and Clinton have prominent noses with fleshy tips that project their personality into the world with emotional sensitivity. Their strong, wide jaws support their desires with a stubborness and a determination to uphold their ideals.

The full lips and large mouth of **Gates** shows his creativity and sensuous appetite for success. The tension in the right corner of his mouth indicates the restraint in expressing all he has on his mind. The smaller right eye shows the shrewd observation of his analytical mind that sizes things up carefully. He has a very good balance in the curved hairline. This makes him broad and open-minded with a great sense of mental adaptability and creative imagination.

Clinton's hairline narrows and is higher on the right than the left creating a restriction and imbalance in left and right brain attitudes to life. The narrowing of the frame of mind on the sides make him at times closed off from others' opinions. This causes an internalising of his emotions, creating self-judgement. Self-sacrificing for the rationality of others and what he must do in service, like Heads of State, he comes off "*second best*". The high set of his ears show how much he listens to the mind.

3.12 Al Gore, with the major portion of the face in the mental and physical zones, shows the physical vitality and determination to support and fulfil what his broad and open mind dictates. The powerful nose shows how the personality is projecting itself straight from the mind and what he feels is right. He is straight forward and forthright, even if at times emotions must step aside for fulfilling justice and ambition. His low-set ears enable him to balance the strong mind with good grounding, giving him a better understanding and a willingness to listen to people. The clean-cut features are best suited for the inner strength that will always be expressed without much restraint.

Part 3 Identification of Potentialities

Structure and Balance = Potential for Performance
Physical Success
Principal Indicators:

a) A major portion of the face should occupy the lower **Zone**. **Physical** success needs sustained strength. When the face is **squarish** they are *down to earth* and get on with the job.
b) Good **width** in this area gives good expression adaptability and support. Physical vitality and conscious enthusiasm are experienced and expressed here.
c) **Balance** and flow between **Left and Right** is necessary for sound judgement.
d) A **prominent Nose** indicates the capacity to *be out there*.
e) A **strong Jaw** gives the determination to be self-supporting
f) **Full Lips** show creativity and sensuous appetite for success.
Note the common factors in all these case studies

3.13 (a) Front: Andre Agassi

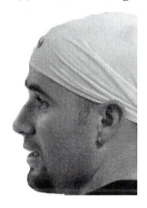

3.13 (b) Profile: Andre Agassi

3.13 Andre Agassi: No1 World class Tennis champion. Each one of the above Principal indicators, a) to f) apply. The quick, strong mind adds a mental clarity, speed and determination to his success. Good balance in the zones and left-right sides with a prominent nose gives him the right structure to achieve top performance.

Principal Indicators
Prominent Features

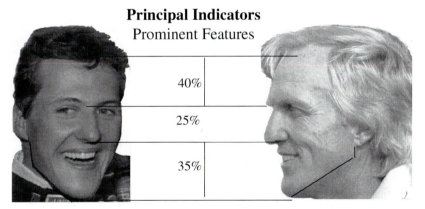

40%

25%

35%

3.14 Front: Schumacher
Racing Car Driver

3.15 Profile: Greg Norman
Champion Golfer

3.14 Front: Schumacher and **3.15 Profile: Greg Norman** both show a very high degree of mental strength, 40%. In the physical zone the very good length from the tip of the nose to the chin shows a great deal of physical vitality and presence. Both have sensitive, tapering jaw lines that indicate the sensitivity and one-pointed focus they both use so well to achieve their sporting goals. Focus on balance is of vital importance.

Face to Face with Facts

Structure and Balance = Potential for Performance
Reliability and Determination
Principal Indicators:

a) A major portion of the face should occupy the lower **Zone.** Physical success needs sustained strength. When the face is **squarish** or **rectangular** they are "down to earth", get on with the job. The more rectangular faces have ideals they will stand up for.

b) **Good width** in this area gives good expression, adaptability and support. Physical vitality and conscious enthusiasm are experienced and expressed here.

c) **Balance** and flow between **Left and Right** is necessary for sound judgement.

d) A **prominent Nose and Cheekbones** indicates the capacity to *"be out there"* and achieve your ambition.

e) A **strong Jaw** gives the determination to be self-supporting.

f) **Full Lips** show creativity and sensuous appetite for success.

Note the common factors in all these case studies

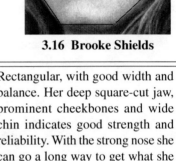

3.16 Brooke Shields

Rectangular, with good width and balance. Her deep square-cut jaw, prominent cheekbones and wide chin indicates good strength and reliability. With the strong nose she can go a long way to get what she wants. It indicates her steadfastness.

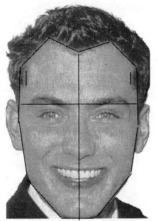

3.17 Jude Law

Principal Indicators
Prominent Features

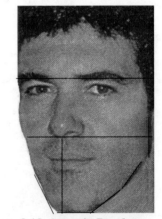

3.18 Antonio Banderas

Determination, strength and open-minded with good balance. Note '"*M*" shaped hairline can create some self-doubt due to past conditioning. The wide nostrils with the tip of the nose pointing down indicate good stamina, a dependability to carry through with good creativity. There is mental determination showing in the greater squareness of the right jaw compared to the left.. The large, open smile in expressing his inner joy for life.

The distance between the nose tip and strong chin containing the warm sensuousness gives him the earthy fullness and *manly* strength. The width in the emotional zone with the strong obvious cheekbones show ambition with a warmth. The dark eyes and bushy eyebrows add to the vitality and passion he emanates. The rebellious hairline adds to the determination to follow through what he sets his heart on.

Part 3 Identification of Potentialities

Structure and Balance = Potential for Performance
Projection of the personality ~ *The Outstanding Profile*

Principal Indicators (ref. 3.4 page 63)

a) Seen in profile look for the **part of the face that is projecting** the personality **forward** into the world more than the rest of the face.

b) Note any part that is **receding** or **withdrawn structurally.** These factors give added information about how this one will experience and apply these characteristics

c) Note the distance between the **tip** of the **nose** and the position where the **ear connects** to the face. This indicates the way they are projecting their own personality forward. The areas of the Zone or zones the ear occupies indicates how we interact in each of those zones. This is determined by the height, size and angle of the ear.

d) Note **where** the bridge of the **nose starts**. When the nose starts from the forehead straight to the tip the ridge divides the face so the person perceives from the mind and heart(eye) is separated from each other. This one may not see *"eye to eye"* with others emotionally and their physical needs.

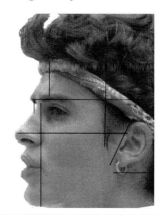

3.19 Sabatini The emotional and physical zones project strongly outward, led by a large *"straight forward"* nose. Note the angle of the ear setting. The ear is set very low. This keeps her in contact with her feelings and has her *"ear to the ground"*. The overhanging brow and deep-set warm brown eyes show an intuition and a quick, observant mind. Her *"hot lips"* express her warm and nurturing soul with a fiery and passionate spirit inside!

3.20 Alan Prost

Principal Indicators
Prominent Features

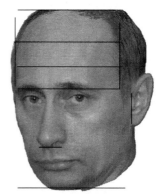

3.21 Putin

The focus and energy is concentrated in the two lower zones. This keeps Alan Prost well focused and physically in contact with high-speed driving. The prominent observation overhanging deep-set eyes maintains clarity while the very strong and sharp nose projects aggressive precision. This is strengthened by the sensitive but protruding chin.	The focus and energy is concentrated in the two upper zones. Putin's very powerful, intuitive, broad and open mind projects all his energy forward. The ear to nose tip distance and large ears give him the energy to be alert, inventive and *"stick his nose out"* into the world with sensitivity, but forcefully. Note his full lips.

Face to Face with Facts

Structure and Balance = Potential for Performance
Creativity ~ Memory ~ Intuition

Principal Indicators

a) The broad open mind has great height and width – broad and open-minded.

b) The forehead overhangs the eyes that are usually deep set for focus and evaluative observation. Memory and observation sections are usually protruding, while the creativity-imagination section is open like a radar dish or has rebellious or unruly hair (the energy to change things).

c) The manifestation of this mental genius must show supportive strength in the emotional and/or physical zones of the face.

d) Creativity shows in the lips, specially in the fullness of the top lip.

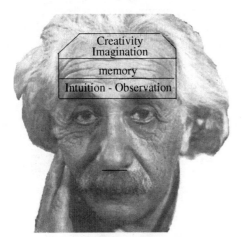
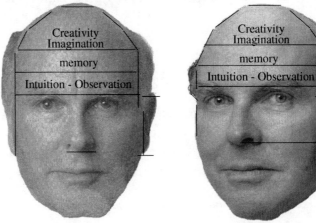

3.22 Albert Einstein
Scientific Revolution also Ref. 3.8 p 66

3.23 Craig Venter: Father of Genome Technology
Genetic Revolution: Human function and health.

3.22 Albert Einstein: Broad, open-minded, protruding forehead the overhangs deep-set searching eyes. The rebellious hairline indicates how he revolutionised so many scientific theories. The long, large protruding nose, with the fleshy tip, ensured that he stuck it out enough to be recognised and accepted, with understanding and sensitivity (fleshy tip). The bushy moustache over the upper lip helps ground these *"theories"* as the gesture indicates " *I must show them how it works*".

3.23 Craig Venter: The vast expansive mental zone shows a very high degree of an open and broad-minded attitude. The whole forehead protrudes and overhangs the deep-set, warm, kind eyes. The mind is quick to observe and intuitive as seen by the protrusion above the eyes. The creative imagination is wide open like a radar dish to accept whatever is out there to listen for. The additional special factors to note are: The distance of the ear connection to the tip of the prominent nose shows the great depth of desire and feeling to put all he has to use. This is enhanced by the large ear that occupies a large part of the emotional and physical zones where he applies his work to life issues and the human factor. The full top lip with a good curve and the point of refinement confirms the intuition and creativity. The large mouth and full bottom lip shows his outspoken attitude. The prominent fleshed cheekbones and a line between the eyebrows that rises upwards shows the he has to achieve at all costs what he sets his mind to. He does this with understanding.

Part 3 Identification of Potentialities

Structure and Balance = Potential for Performance
Self Control and Spontaneity
Principal Indicators

a) **Self-control** is the mind resisting the **spontaneity** that come from the heart, expressed with this inner sense of joy in expressing the self. This **resistance** will be noticed in the tightness of the **jaw** resulting in the compression of the lips.

b) Self-control may also be noticed in the straightness or forced lowering of the **eyebrows** to shut feelings of emotions, or internalise them.

c) **Spontaneity** is the innocent expression of joyful feelings set free to express themselves without judgement of the conscious mind. This will be indicated by arched **eyebrows,** open **eyes** and a natural large **smile** from usually full, relaxed **lips.** There will be a sparkle in the **eyes** and a relaxed **jaw**.

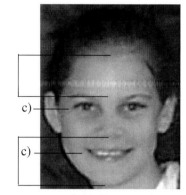

3.24 Spontaneity

c) Spontaneity is seen in the relaxed smile and gentleness of the eyes. The eyebrows are full and set well apart giving freer expression to her identity. The width of the face and full cheeks show the fullness of affection and feelings. The strong mind is in the large, high forehead.

Principal Indicators
Prominent Features

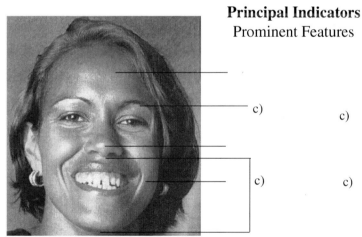

3.25 Cathy Freeman

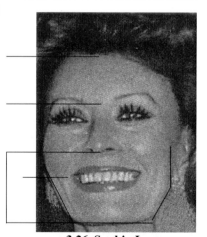

3.26 Sophia Loren

| 3.25 Cathy Freeman: The full lips in an open smile, c), with the curved raised eyebrows shows the warmth of her heart that shows through the brown eyes. The fleshy cheeks and wide, soft-tipped nose confirm this. However, the tighter and smaller left side of the whole face shows an emotional control of her inner feelings. Notice the smaller left eye. The large open forehead with a curved hairline speaks for one with an open frame of mind, and a wide jaw to support it. | 3.26 Sophia Loren: The large, flashing smile and full, voluptuous lips give Sophia Loren a passionate expression of warmth, especially when supported by the brown eyes. The wide jaw and broad chin show a strength and self-control that lets you know she is in charge of her affairs. With the major part of her energy in the physical and emotional zones she emanates an earthy sensuality. The fleshed, prominent cheek bones help her achieve her ambitions with feeling. |

Face to Face with Facts

Structure and Balance = Potential for Performance
Love and Sensuality

Principal Indicators ~ The Eyes and Lips

a) **The Eyes** express the sensitivity of the **heart**, large, open and balanced or restrained.
b) **The Lips**, full and sensuous, is the warmth of the **womb** that creates and nurtures life, as a woman does. A natural large **smile** from full, relaxed **lips** births the love for life.
c) Note the **development** and **fleshiness** in the emotional and physical zone.
d) Bushy **eyebrows** add energy and earthiness to the heart.
e) **Symmetrical curves** of face shape, eyebrows, eyes and lips show change and flow of energy with flexibility.
f) **Fringes** and hair draped across the forehead enhances the feminine by covering or internalising the thoughts.
g) The **delicate nose** narrowing at the nostrils show a subdued sense of personal identity.
h) A **longer nose** with the **tip pointed** to the **upper lip** enhances the degree of sensual and creative energy.

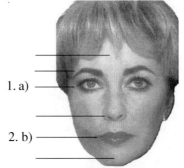

3.27 Elizabeth Taylor

a) Beautiful, open, well-balanced eyes, affectionate; could be a bit too trusting.
b) Full sensuous, warm and nurturing.
c) Full and earthy in the emotional zone.
d) Bushy eyebrows enhance the eyes.
e) The soft curves of the face lines, eyes and nostrils indicate a sensitivity that is easily moved or effected by others' needs.
f) The fringe is designed to soften the strong mind that is very dominant This mental energy flows into the jaws, showing some stubborness and control.
g) The nose is narrow at the base showing some lack of personal identity and self-worth. The wide bridge defuses her focus.

Principal Indicators
Prominent Features

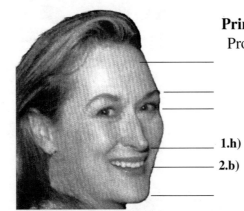

3.28 Meryl Streep – Sensuous ambition.

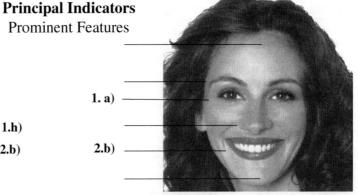

3.29 Julia Roberts – Sensuous warmth.

3.28 Meryl Streep: 1.h) - 2.b) Her prominent nose enhances her creativity and sensuality, especially when she smiles. The large mouth supports this warm, nurturing feminine energy. The large sloping forehead shows the strong, open and quick mind. The high cheekbones and strong chin supports the determination to fulfil her ambitions. The curved eyebrows, d) indicate an open attitude to life that she observes with a careful, deep focus. At times this can make her hard on herself and expect too much perfection.

3.29 Julia Roberts: 1.a) - 2.b) The large, warm, sparkling brown eyes emanating the love that flows so freely from her soul is simultaneously supported by a large sensuous mouth. The flare of the nostrils when she smiles has an endearing trust-worthiness and passion that is comforting.
d) - e) The large curved eyebrows enhance the power in the eyes. The right eye slopes down slightly towards the nose. This is inherited criticism she may now be using on herself. She needs more self-acknowledgment of her soul.

Part 3 Identification of Potentialities

Structure and Balance = Potential for Performance
Health, Vitality and Longevity

Principal Indicators

a) **Health** and **vitality** are present when there is a good balance in all three Zones.
b) **Wide nostrils** also add vitality to the physical strength. They indicate an honest and dependable person with ample stamina.
c) **Longevity** is indicated by the length of the **distance between** the **nose tip** and the **chin.** The larger and wider the physical zone is the greater the physical capabilities and enduring good health.
d) A large **mental zone** with a delicate tapering **physical** zone indicates that this person is a **sensitive** intellectual that needs to watch his physical vitality so that stress does not cause *"burnout"*.
e) The **size** and **position** of the **ears**, when they are in the lower two zones, add to the physical vitality and stability of the person. When they are large and fleshy they are listening to the emotional and physical needs.

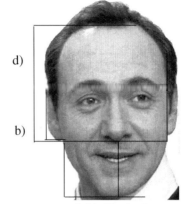
3.30 Kevin Spacey

3.30 Kevin Spacey has high mental energy and a delicate ,sensitive, physical zone that could cause stress through too much pressure to get ahead. The large ears and emotional sensitivity will help him to bring balance in health and vitality. The large nose, wide nostrils and full lips will sustain his vitality. The nose also indicates that he is honest and dependable.

Principal Indicators
Prominent Features

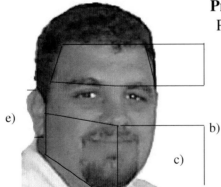
3.31 Shane Sullivan

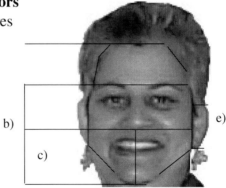
3.32 Gillian Maddigan

3. 31 Shane Sullivan: Vitality and a long life is seen here in the large fleshy area in depth and height of the physical zone. This is enhanced by the size and position of the ears in the emotional and physical zones. The soft-tipped nose and large nostrils indicate an honest and dependable person. It also adds to the physical energy available. The sloping eyes show compassion. The frame of mind shows some internalising of personal emotional feelings as is also seen by some restriction on the left side of the face.	3.32 Gillian Maddigan: The emotional and physical zones occupy a major portion of the face. This highly sensitive person with ample physical energy and vitality is substantiated by the length between the nose tip and chin. This reassures long life and good health. The large fleshy ears hung halfway between the two lower zones adds to the earthy aspirations. The high but tapering forehead and protruding fleshy chin indicate a strong and quick mind. The frame of mind closes in indicating a degree of internalising feelings.

Structure and Balance = Potential for Performance Happiness and Emotional Stability

Principal Indicators

a) **The Eyes** express the sensitivity of the **heart,** large, open and balanced or restrained. Note: The presence of **happiness** is seen in the **sparkle**, fullness and relaxed **muscles** around the **eyes.**

b) The *"longing"* for happiness look is seen in the slight **caution** around the eyes, usually in **deep-set eyes.**

c) The touch of **sadness**, knowing what love and happiness feels like inside but *can't quite grasp it*!

d) **The Lips**, full and sensuous, expressing the warmth of nurturing, with a natural large **smile** from full, relaxed **lips** that births the love for life.

c) Note the **development, width** and **fleshiness** in the emotional and physical Zone.

d) The **structure** of the **jaw** and **chin** are essential factors for **stability** and **support** for the emotions. A wide jaw or broad chin show support relative to the degree of width. A tapering jaw or chin shows a good sensitivity. This one must stay centred and grounded.

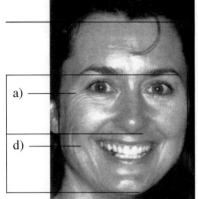

3.33 Jane Easson

3.33 Jane Esson: The good width and height of the two lower zones is full of warmth, love and spontaneous joy in the wide-open smile. The width at the jaw shows a great tenaciousness that, at times, could hurt herself when her expectations are not met. The large eyes and mouth with a ready smile express her true nature readily.

Principal Indicators
Prominent Features

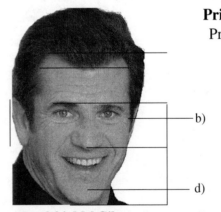

3.34 Mel Gibson

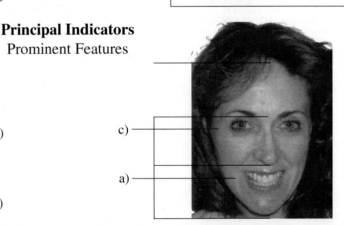

3.35 Victoria

3.34 Mel Gibson: The compassionate blue eyes have the "*longing look*" that watch carefully from under overhanging brows. The sensitive tapering physical zone shows a sensitivity that is supported by a strong, wide chin. The flaring nostrils with the tip of the nose pointing down gives Mel Gibson that ravenous, sexy look of attraction. The "*M*" shaped hairline shows great creativity that at time creates self-doubt. The large ears connect him well to all three zones.

3.35 Victoria: The long face with a delicate, tapering jaw and chin shows a very sensitive person with very broad and open mind. The beautiful eyes and large relaxed mouth are very expressive, a great creative sensitivity enhanced by the large curving eyebrows with a passion for whatever she does. The low delicate energy in the physical area shows grounding is essential to avoid the disappointment that shows in the eyes. The soft tip of the nose shows her gentleness.

Part 4
Case Studies of Notable Personalities

Mother Teresa

Bob Ansett

Bill Clinton

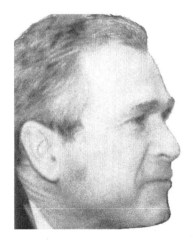

George Bush

With
A Comparative Study
of
Adolf Hitler

Princess Diana

Face to Face with Facts

How to Read a Face
Follow the Basic Principles of Energy Flow
Parts 1 and 2 gives all the information you need to read a face

Total focus on the face, Face the Facts that are being presented. Be systematic, follow the procedure suggested. Understanding and compassion are essential. Notice the obvious signs and disregard minor details, they will balance out.

The Face at a Glance

Overall Face Shape – Front: The Blueprint of the Soul	Basic shapes and combinations:– Square, oval, etc. Note the shape may vary in a particular zone.
Personality Projection – Profile: Special structural potentials	Portions of the face, zone or individual part, that projects forward or is pulled back is of significance.
Most Prominent Feature: Special feature of strength	What jumps out to be noticed at first glance. The individual part that stands out strongly.
Three Major Zones: Distribution for life's purpose	The proportions of Mental Emotional and Physical energy indicate potentials for performance in life.
Right/Left Balance: Internal consciousness externalised	Left/Right brain balance is essential for efficient performance. The two halves must fit well together.
R/L: Balance of each sense: The response to life's conditions	Each of the individual parts indicate their potential function or suppression. They need to do so equally.
The Hair and Lines on the face They show sensitivity and maturity.	Hair growth and lines of experience add additional information on personality performance.

Evaluation

Points to Incorporate: **1. Total focus** and full eye-to-eye contact with touch is essential. **2. Truthfully** expressing your observations will benefit the most. **3. An Evaluation** means that you are showing them some useful potentials that were not noticed.	Touch, voice tone and a straight-forward approach will create confidence and trust. The most important benefit for the person is to be understood in a way they know themselves but is seldom noticed by others truthfully. This confirmation creates a tool of valuable communication for both the reader and the person whose face is being read. Show you care to spend this valuable opportunity to understand them because they are worth it. Give them their due recognition. This is an excellent opportunity to integrate this.

Part 4: Case Studies of Notable Personalities

Case Study 4.1 Mother Teresa

The Face at a Glance

Overall Face Shape – Front:	Rectangle/Triangle, very high humanitarian ideals, emotionally and physically sensitive to uphold them.
Personality Projection – Profile:	Mid Zone, Nose and Cheekbones – achieve ambition.
Most Prominent Feature:	A wide, strong **Nose**. Ready to stick it out to get what she set her mind on. Honest, gentle and dependable.
Three Major Zones:	Physical and emotional zone. Long life of very hard work. Great vitality and understanding of people.
Right/Left Balance:	Good balance, slight holding back of personal needs.
R/L: Balance of each sense:	Left eye and corner of the mouth show her personal emotional restraint with the strong mind dominating.

Evaluation

Mother Teresa's face shows all her energy was devoted to the emotional and physical service of mankind. With the head covered constantly with the blue and white habit, it signified her own mind was shut off by the need for service. The faraway look in her eyes were focused on a higher cause a long way from her personal needs. The prominent nose and cheekbones projected her personality with such determination that she went where intended and got what her heart wanted with the softness and subtle gentleness of the fleshy tip on the nose. The double success lines that surround her nose-mouth area show, when she smiled, she achieved what she wanted and followed the deep inner voice of her creative soul. The sloping eyebrows show a deep sense of devotion, looking up to a cause higher than her own. Her left, emotional side, of her whole face shows less energy.
The smaller left eye and the tighter left corner of her mouth show the restraint and control of her personal feelings that may have been suppressed for the purpose of following the strong mind that drove her to keep pursuing her intent silently but relentlessly.

Face to Face with Facts

Case Study 4.2 Princess Diana

The Face at a Glance

Overall Face Shape – Front:	Oval/squarish, with a width in the emotional and the curve in the physical; shows flexibility with warmth.
Personality Projection – Profile:	Mid Zone, Nose and Jawbones – outgoing personality.
Most Prominent Feature:	A strong **Nose** with a good base. Ready to stick it out to project her personal identity and her ideals.
Three Major Zones:	Emotional zone. Wide with straight sides show that she actively pursued what she set her heart on.
Right/Left Balance:	Good balance, left eye slightly guarding emotions.
R/L: Balance of each sense	Tension around the left eye and corner of the mouth show her restraint in expressing personal emotions.

Evaluation

Princess Diana's face shows a warmth and charm that is evident in the wide emotional zone supported by a firm jaw. The width of the face itself personifies the depth with which she expressed her feelings in a practical way. The strong, straight nose made her go out there, be seen, accountable and create a identity of her own. The somewhat boomerang eyebrows express her independence and strength of will. They tend to come down a little low over her guarded eyes that express a lot of love outwardly but hold her own personal feelings inside. The good balance in her face conveys a sense of trust and openness that made her so popular. The hair worn to cover a portion of her forehead expresses her desire to come across more as a warm, affectionate person rather than one with a mind of her own. The strength of the mind and will, however, can be seen in the firm, wide jaw that could firmly support what she wanted. The large mouth and soft, full lips show a warmth and caring nature so sought after, and endeared her to so many. Behind all this, there is a light in the eyes that is yearning for a love and understanding she gave out, but did not get.

Part 4: Case Studies of Notable Personalities

Case Study 4.3 Bill Clinton

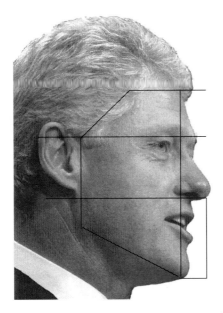

The Face at a Glance

Overall Face Shape – Front:	Rectangle/oval: High ideals, emotionally sensitive, he is determined to represent and fulfil these concepts.
Personality Projection – Profile:	Both lower Zones: Nose and Jaw – supports identity.
Most Prominent Feature:	A projecting **Nose** with **High-set Ears**. Projects his identity forward strongly, listens to his own mind.
Three Major Zones:	70% in the two lower zones. Acts with strength, determination and understanding, Mentally analytical
Right/Left Balance:	Fairly good balance, except in the mental zone.
R/L: Balance of each sense	Hairline drops at the left showing internalising some of his personal feelings due to past conditioning.

Evaluation

Bill Clinton's face **up-front,** would not tell you much about his true blue character as seen in profile. His "*pro-file*" is his pro-fessional file of how he really functions. On the face of things Bill Clinton appears a warm, sensitive man with high ideals (rectangular/oval) and great vitality (wide face and strong jaw), to adapt to the immense task of two terms as President of the United States. The diplomatic (fleshy chin and nose tip) yet resolute determination to have his way supported him a long way in achieving his responsibilities. The hairline, lower on the left than the right says, "I don't think I should tell them how I really feel. They would never understand". **In profile** it is significant to note that the high position of his ear shows how carefully he listens to the internal working of his own mind. Contrary to the softness he shows up front, the profile shows the power with which he projects his personality out there (prominent nose), relentlessly supported by an inner tenacity and determination, (deep jaw, protruding chin and lower portion of the face). This give us the awareness of the difference between Bill as a human being and Bill as a President!

Case Study 4.4 Bob Ansett

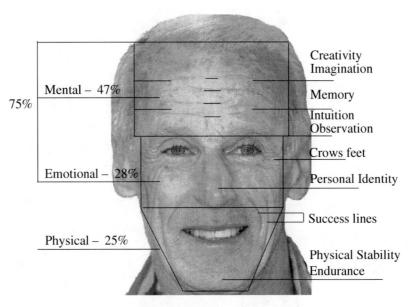

The Face at a Glance

Overall Face Shape – Front:	Rectangle – Triangle: Great vision and creativity with stability to fulfil his passion to achieve his goals.
Personality Projection – Profile:	Strong **Nose** and **Chin** willing to take risks.
Most Prominent Feature:	Forehead – Broad and open-minded. The creativity and imagination section is wide and open to new ideas.
Three Major Zones:	47% in the mental zone shows the powerful mind was able to channel all his desires (28%) to fulfil his vision.
Right/Left Balance:	Good balance – The right mid-zone slightly smaller.
R/L: Balance of each sense	Good balance – The right eye is slightly smaller, the cheek and the corner of the mouth shows the same careful focus and caution in decision making.

Evaluation

The face of **Bob Ansett** shows good balance, with a rectangular face-shape of one who has great ideals with the creativity, intuition and motivation to fulfil these concepts. Even with a triangular base there is good depth between nose tip and a wide chin that gives him the sensitivity to "*swing with the needs of the times*" with vitality, stability and resilience. This is accentuated by the many successful development lines his face carries. The well-developed cheek lines (ref. page 57 #2.109), rising "*crow's feet*" at the eyes, and four well-defined forehead lines of intuition, communication, warmth and ambition tell the tale of his sustained success. The blue eyes show an understanding that still carry the sparkle of a soul's mission accomplished with a smile that has had the "*sweet taste of success*". There are many lines of life's challenges on his face, that are surpassed by his ability to literally "*keep his ears pricked up*" for trouble or opportunities that came along. This is seen in his large protruding ears set a little high, connecting the mental and emotional zones, listening to the inner workings of the mind that does not give away too much.

Part 4: Case Studies of Notable Personalities

Case Study 4.5 George Bush

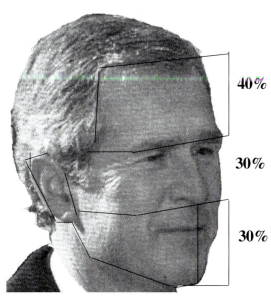
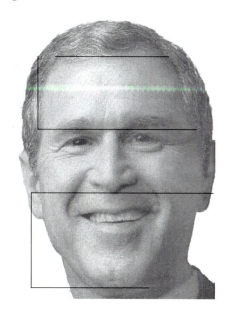

40%

30%

30%

The Face at a Glance

Overall Face Shape – Front:	Rectangle – Oval: High ideals with the flexibility and sensitivity to deal with issues of power or control.
Personality Projection – Profile:	Physical emotional zones push forward.
Most Prominent Feature:	Nose points down, large sloping ear.
Three Major Zones:	40% mental, 30% emotional, 30% physical zone. The good length from nose tip to chin – good vitality
Right/Left Balance:	Well-balanced face – shows a balanced outlook.
R/L: Balance of each sense	Good balance – The right eye is slightly smaller, the large ears slope back further away from emotions.

Evaluation

President George Bush shows us more about himself in this semi-profile shot than a full frontal. When we notice the large sloping ear and the nose tip pointing down we see the special features behind the face of this flexible, affable person with high ideals. The nose pointing down (intuition and creativity), to a "*stiff upper lip*" that matches the rectangular hairline (somewhat fixed frame of mind) speaks volumes of his conservative attitude and upbringing. The large ears sloping back match the guarded eyes that show how much goes on inside his mind and how guarded he is about showing his true feelings. Like a "*born diplomat*" he will tell you what you need to know and work the rest out himself. On the face of it all he shows a cute boyish simplicity with plenty of vitality (note: the nose-tip – chin distance) and enthusiasm in his bushy eyebrows. The depth of the physical zone with its oval shape, along with the ear lobes also in this area, show his ability to work well with others. He is willing to delegate responsibility and apply himself with great understanding of people's needs. This flexibility is seen in the oval shape of the two lower zones.

Face to Face with Facts

Case Study 4.6: The Two Faces of Adolf Hitler

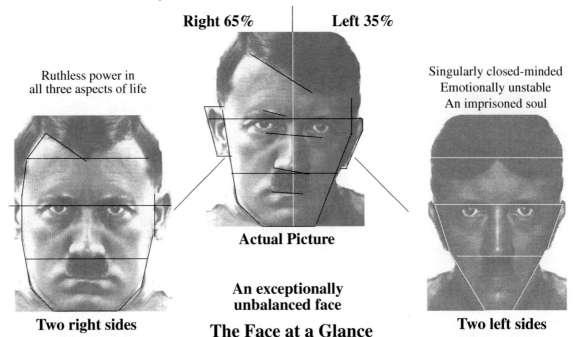

Right 65% | **Left 35%**

Ruthless power in all three aspects of life

Singularly closed-minded
Emotionally unstable
An imprisoned soul

Actual Picture

An exceptionally unbalanced face

Two right sides — **The Face at a Glance** — **Two left sides**

Overall Face Shape – Front:	Rectangle on right – Triangle on left. Great diversity in all three zones. Imbalance structure=performance.
Personality Projection – Profile:	Physically and mentally forceful, pushing forward.
Most Prominent Feature:	The exceptional imbalance of the two sides show the left sensitive side dominated by the will.
Three Major Zones:	**Right** 45% – 32% – 28% / **Left** 32% – 55% – 23%. Too much internal conflict to think or feel clearly.
Right/Left Balance:	Exceptional imbalance: Right 65% – Left 35%.
R/L: Balance of each sense	Note all five senses and the mind are pulled up sharply with strength on the right and depressed on the left.

Evaluation

Adolf Hitler – A strong soul that came into this world to learn to balance power with sensitivity to create the perfect human. His own internal struggle to find this lost battle of balance was externalised. Power slowly crushed the sensitivity and left the soul trapped deep in darkness. (Note the overpowering right side brought to light while the fragile left is so dark.) So engulfing was the imbalance fed by thousands of countrymen surrendering their souls to him in bondage that feed the egotistic personality. This internal imbalance engulfed the world. The face has been so twisted out of shape that it personified his attitude in life. The whites under the eyes show a loss of contact with the reality of life. The twisted wide nose with the squat moustache only under the nose enhances this fiery ego. The stubborn jaw holds fast any resolution his strong imaginative mind envisioned. At times that nervous little depressed soul escaped to express its terror and depression. This was so misunderstood by those that surrounded him. The unpredictable decisions and behaviour was the expression of his own loss of control over himself, until he became his own prisoner.

Part 4: Case Studies of Notable Personalities

"FACE THESE FACTS"

Mother Teresa – Sacrifice of the self to the higher calling of the soul for service to others. This powerful soul directed her inner power and all the power that others empowered her with towards the service of others. She utilised everything she had to empower the have-nots. The balance in her structure sustained her with strength, fulfilling her life's purpose with love.

Princess Diana – Charming, with clear-cut features of a love and warmth she emanated, is so dearly sought after in any part of the world. Her popularity stemmed from the sensitive quality of strength she showed – to acknowledge the need of others at their level. The impression she left behind said with love and simplicity that we are human beings. This was her soul's purpose.

Ex-President **Bill Clinton** with the true qualities of a diplomat showed how he was built to project his inner strength when, on the face of it, was not noticed. Internalising his thoughts he pushed forward in the face of petty bickering to fulfil the convictions and responsibilities of his office. He stayed focused on the *"big picture"* with the dignity of a soul with high ideals.

Bob Ansett, with the great creative mind used with balance, shows the qualities of his inner self being expressed without much conflict. There is a lot of thinking behind the compassionate yet calculating eyes. The many development lines showing, indicate that he has been innovative in the face of many challenges and has grown successful from them.

President **George Bush** with a wide, open forehead sloping eyebrows and guarded eyes shows the world what he wants them to see. He is open-minded with a squarish frame, indicating a degree of fixity of concepts. He has good balance in the left and right sides and an oval shape in the lower part of the face. This shows flexibility and his ability to delegate power and deal with humanitarian issues well, even with a conservative point of view.

Adolf Hitler – The great imbalance he portrays was overlooked as we got caught up in the events, not the cause of the events. How much pain must we endure before we look at what is staring at us in the face. The imbalance of structure destroyed the infrastructure of life itself – internally and externally.

"Who have you given so much of your energy and support to rule your world?"
"Have you studied their face before surrendering your trust?"

"FACE TO FACE WITH FACTS"

Now it is time to ask ourselves some very personal questions.

The evidence and facts are looking at us *"In the Face"*.

1. Are we prepared to look at our own faces and notice how we are facing life?

2. Are we prepared to admit that only what we have is what we have got to work with?

3. Are we prepared to look at our own experience of the world, not the world as our experience?

4. Are we willing to correct these to bring balance to our own experiences or embroil the world so our experiences would be correct?

5. Would it not be easier for ourselves to bring balance in just our **own being** (the only **one** that is our own), rather than change so many others so we feel balanced? Life may be easier this way.

6. Are we willing to fulfil our soul's sole purpose to bring more fulfilment into its own world?

7. Are we willing to consider that freedom, personal identity, confidence in the self and individuality of the soul are some of the greatest values of integrity in life that we love?

Now Consider These Facts

1. Structure = Performance ~ Balance = Positive results.
2. Structure = Sacred Geometry = Direction of energy flow = How thought directs energy.
3. One single Soul comes into being, in a body creating Duality or "Identity" = **"Id"** and **"Entity"**
4. This duality is personified throughout the bodily experience and **shows** its **duality** in the **face**.
5. Our sole life's purpose is to evolve into greater balance through our own life experiences.
6. This evolution is a continuing process of learning for everyone of us, and will continue to be.
7. We must accept our **innocence** and listen to this **inner-sense** to accept others in the same way.

Communication is the Key ~
Freedom and Love is the Experience

Communication ~ Balance ~ Understanding

Understand yourself so you may understand others.

Know that you are worthy of the attention you did not get.

Give others a few minutes of undivided attention they have never experienced.

Look at a person straight in the face with the care and interest they seldom, have received, with the beauty and love that you feel in you.

Your world and the world out there will never look or feel the same as you practice *"The Art of Reading Faces"*.

Conclusion

The Purpose of this Book

I honour and give thanks to every face in this book that shall teach us so much about life as they show us how they lived theirs. I have brought together the faces of real people. As I have studied each one of them they have added so much more to what I have learnt in reading thousands of faces professionally and teaching this art as a subject.

I have placed my love and passion for accepting people with an open mind above all things. This has opened my heart. Experience this opportunity to enrich each other with the understanding of one soul with another. Enjoy yourself by rising above the clouds of conditioned living.

"This Art of Reading Faces" is to evaluate your experience of others and yourself. Add something positive to each experience, enriching the event with your compassion and understanding. The reason we have come together must be for the purpose of learning something from the experience. Look at their positive achievements and the potential they may have to improve their self worth by acknowledging them.

Remember every soul is a spiritual being endeavouring with its own "inner-sense" to find more balance. There is a lesson and a learning in every experience. Honour the effort of learning of others, as you do for yourself.

Hermann

Part 4: Case Studies of Notable Personalities

A Sketch by my Father

Mother Mary – Mother of Compassion

"Look upon each other with the love, understanding and the sweet innocence of the child we are, that untarnished soul. She waits patiently for you to recognise her for who she is".

"Is not **Love, Living Love?**"

Summary

Charts and Case Studies

1.1	Chart: Front View – Facing the World	6
1.2	Chart: Profile – Projecting the Personality into the World	6
1.19	Chart: Three Zones and the Body in the Face	11
1.20	Case Study: Sizing up the Face at a Glance	12
1.21	Chart: Overall Face Shapes	13
1.32	Case Study: A Sample Reading at First Glance	17
1.33	Case Study: Fleshing Out The Framework	18
1.34	A Sample Reading at First Glance	18
3.2	Chart: Structure and Balance	62
3.5	Case Study: The Two Faces of Abraham Lincoln	64
3.6	Case Study: Slobodan Milosovic – The Potential for Performance	65
3.9	Case Study: Alan Bond – Imbalance Structure	67
3.10	Case Study: Financial and Administrative Success – Bill Gates	68
3.11	Case Study: Financial and Administrative Success – Bill Clinton	68
3.12	Case Study: Financial and Administrative Success – Al Gore	68
3.22	Case Study: Creativity ~ Memory ~ Intuition – Albert Einstein	72
3.23	Case Study: Creativity ~ Memory ~ Intuition – Craig Venter	72
Chart	How to Read a Face	78
4.1	Case Study: Mother Teresa	79
4.2	Case Study: Princess Diana	80
4.3	Case Study: Bill Clinton	81
4.4	Case Study: Bob Ansett	82
4.5	Case Study: George Bush	83
4.6	Case Study: Adolf Hitler	84
Chart	Face These Facts	85

Appendix

Ref. No	Title	Page
Part 1:		
The Art of Reading Faces		
1.1	Facing the World – Front View	6
1.2	Profile ~ Projecting the Personality into the World	6
Overall Structure and Face Shapes		
1.3	Round	7
1.4	Oval	7
1.5	Square	7
1.6	Rectangular	8
1.7	Triangular – Upright	8
1.8	Triangular – Inverted	8
Combinations of some of the above basic types		
1.9	Combination of Figure 1.6 and Figure 1.8	8
1.10	Combination of Figure 1.5 and Figure 1.4	9
1.11	Combination Figure 1.7 and Figure 1.5	9
Fundamentals of Basic Settings and Lines – Tell-Tale Lines		
1.12	Straight Lines	9
1.13	Curved Lines	9
1.14	Right Angular Lines	10
1.15	Descending and Drooping Lines	10
1.16	Descending Lines Come Together	10
1.17	Rising, Uplifting Lines	10
1.18	Eyebrow Pointed	10
The Three Zones – Mental, Emotional and Physical		
1.19	Three Zones and the Body in the Face	11
1.20	Sizing up the Face at a glance	12
1.21	A Comparative Chart of Overall Face Shapes	13
Basic Structures & Combinations Fleshing Out The Framework		
1.22	The face– 27 Muscles	14

Ref. No	Title	Page
Common Characteristics of Basic Face Shapes		
1.23	Apollo	14
1.24	Jupiter	14
1.25	Neptune	15
1.26	Mars	15
1.27	Venus	15
1.28	Mercury	16
1.29	Saturn	16
1.30	Uranus	16
1.31	Pluto	17
Sample Reading at First Glance –		
1.32	Mars/Mercury/Saturn	17
Fleshing Out The Framework		
1.33	Case Study	18
Sample Reading at First Glance –		
1.34	Jupiter/Mercury	18
Part 2:		
Assessment of Individual Parts Facing the World		
Sample Readings at First Glance		
2.1	Alan Bond	21
2.2	Princess Diana	21
The Forehead – The Frame of the Mind Front View		
2.3	The Height/Width	22
2.3a	Broad and Open-minded	22
2.4	The Three Regions – Forehead	22
2.4a	Dominant Observation	22
2.4b	Dominant Creativity	22
The Forehead The Frame of the Mind In Profile		
2.5	Creative/Imagination	23
2.6	Observant/Intuitive	23
2.7	Memory/Analytical	23

Ref. No	Title	Page	Ref. No	Title	Page

The Forehead ~ The Frame of the Mind
The Hairline
2.8   The Frame of the Mind   24
2.9   Straight, Broad and Wide   24
2.10   Straight, Narrow and Wide   24
2.11   Straight, Narrow and Short   25
2.12   Broad, Open and Rounded   25
2.13   Peaked   25
2.14   "*M*" Shaped, the Widow's Peak   26
2.15   Jagged Hairline   26
2.16   Combination   26

The Hair Length
2.17a&b   Long hair   27
2.17c   Short hair or a shaved   27

The Hair Type
2.18   Fringes   28
2.18a   Fringe   28
2.18b   No Fringe   28

The Eyebrows ~ Communication
The Eyebrow Type
2.19a   The Eyebrows   29
2.19b   Well-Balanced Eyebrows   29
2.20   Boomerang   29
2.21   Low-Set Eyebrows   29

The Eyebrows Set
2.22   Very High-Set Eyebrows   30
2.23   Straight Eyebrows   30
2.24   Sloping Upwards   30
2.25   Curve Downwards   30

The Eyebrows ~ Communication
The Eyebrow Hairs
2.26   Growing Upwards   31
2.27   Grow Downward   31
2.28   Thin or Scanty Eyebrows   31
2.29   Thick, Bushy Eyebrows   31

The Eyebrow Position
2.30   Joined Eyebrows   32
2.31   Sympathetic Eyebrows   32
2.32   Acuity of Vision   32

The Eyes ~ A Point of View
The Eye Types
2.33   Eyes represent the Heart   33

Eye Set
2.34   Good Balance – Understanding   33
2.35   Wider Apart   33

Eye Set
2.36   Set Close together   34
2.37   Deep-Set eyes   34
2.38   Protruding eyes   34

Eyes Levels
2.39   Eyes Levels   35
2.40   Eyes slope upwards   35
2.41   Eyes slope downwards   35

Size of Eyes
2.42   Large eyes   36
2.43   Small eyes   36

Floating Irises
2.44   Whites show   36
2.45   Irises sink too low   36

Eye Colour   37

The Nose ~ The Size of the Nose
The Personality Knows
2.46   The Nose   38
2.47   A Well-balanced   38
2.48   A Long-nosed   38
2.49   Long, narrow nose   39
2.50   A Broad nose   39
2.51   A Large nose   39
2.52   A Prominent Arched nose   40
2.53   Short nose   40
2.54   A Snub nose   40

Nose Bridges
2.55   Starts from forehead   41
2.56   Starts between the eyes   41

Nose Ridge
2.57   Slim – prominent and arched or wide and strong   41

Ref. No	Title	Page	Ref. No	Title	Page

The Nose ~ The Size of the Nose
The Personality Knows
Tip of the Nose
2.58 Soft fleshy tip   42
2.59 Pointed tip   42
2.60 Grooved   42

Shape of the Nostrils
2.61 Flattened wings   42
2.62 Square nostrils   42

The Ear
Listening Carefully to Reality
Ear Function
2.63 The Ear Zones   43
2.64 The Ridge and Cup   43
2.65 The Intuitive Ear   43

Ear Size
2.66 Large ears   44
2.67 Medium sized   44
2.68 Small ears   44

Ear Settings
2.69 Touching all three zones   45
2.70 Low set   45
2.69 High set   45
2.72 Set far back   46
2.73 Ears stick out   46

Ear Lobes
2.74 Large long lobes   46
2.75 Without lobes   46

Cheeks and Cheekbones
Ambition/Cheekiness
Types of Cheekbones
2.76 Bony – visible   47
2.77 High – fleshy   47
2.78 High – flat   47

The Cheeks
2.79 Full, chubby cheeks   48
2.80 Lean cheeks   48

The Mouth and Lips
A Taste for Life
Types of Mouths
2.81 Balanced Mouth   49
2.82 Large Mouth   49
2.83 Small Mouth   49

Types of Lips
2.84 Thin lips   50
2.85 Straight line   50
2.86 Curving-up line   50
2.87 The point of sensitivity   51
2.88 The point of refinement   51
2.89 Sensuous top lip   51
2.90 Vocal lower lip   51

The Jaw
The Foundation of Life
Types of Jaws
2.91 A Wide jaw   52
2.92 A Deep jaw   52
2.93 A Curved jawbone   52

The Chin
The Support of Life
Types of Chins
2.94 Weak receding chin   53
2.95 Jutting forward chin   53
2.96 A pointed chin   53
2.97 A wide chin
 53

The Lines of Development
The Tell-Tale Lines
Thinking Lines
2.98 a &b Forehead – Thinking Lines   54

Lines of Focus
2.99   Single   55
2.100   Two parallel   55
2.101   Three vertical lines   55
2.102   Slope inwards   55
2.103   Lines bend   55

Ref. No	Title	Page	Ref. No	Title	Page

The Lines of Development
The Tell-Tale Lines
Crow's Feet
2.104	Curve upward	56
2.105	Curve downward	56
2.106	Crossing lines	56

Cheek Lines
2.107	Cheek lines	57
2.108	Two drop lines	57
2.109	Second set – cheek lines	57
2.110	Mandarin	57

Facial Hair
Vitality and Sensitivity
Hair on the Face
2.111	Facial Hair	58

Moustache
2.112	Short and squat	58
2.113	Open	58
2.114	Pointed and up	58
2.114a	Sideburns	59
2.114b	Beards – Full	59
2.115	Beards – Pointed or tailored	59

Part 3:
Identification of Potential Characteristics
3.1	Skeletal Structure = Geometric Energy Flow	61
3.2	Structure and Balance Compare right ~ left	62
3.3	Face in Front View	63
3.4	Face in Profile	63
3.5	Case Study: Abraham Lincoln	64
3.6	Case Study: Slobodan Milosevic	65
3.7	High intellect	66
3.8	Einstein ~ Intellect	66
3.9	Case Study: Alan Bond	67
3.10	Case Study: Bill Gates	68
3.11	Case Study: Bill Clinton	68
3.12	Case Study: Al Gore	68

Identification of Potential Characteristics
Physical Success
3.13a	Andre Agassi – Front	69
3.13b	Andre Agassi – Profile	69
3.14	Schumacher – Front	69
3.15	Greg Norman – Profile	69

Reliability and Determination
3.16	Brooke Shields	70
3.17	Jude Law	70
3.18	Antonio Banderas	70

Projection of the personality
3.19	Sabatini	71
3.20	Alan Prost	71
3.21	Putin	71

Creativity ~ Memory ~ Intuition
3.22	Albert Einstein	72
3.23	Craig Venter	72

Self Control and Spontaneity
3.25	Cathy Freeman	73
3.26	Sophia Loren	73

Love and Sensuality
3.27	Elizabeth Taylor	74
3.28	Meryl Streep	74
3.29	Julia Roberts	74

Health, Vitality and Longevity
3.30	Kevin Spacey	75
3.31	Shane Sullivan	75
3.32	Gillian Maddigan	75

Happiness and Emotional Stability
3.33	Jane Easson	76
3.34	Mel Gibson	76
3.35	Victoria	76

Part 4:
Case Studies of Notable Personalities
Refer Charts and Case Studies

Chart Index

ISBN 155395354-1
9 781553 953548